BALA
THE TI
OF CHANGE

Eight Keys to Collaborative Educational Renewal

Russell T. Osguthorpe
Robert S. Patterson

CORWIN PRESS, INC.
A Sage Publications Company
Thousand Oaks, California

For information:

Corwin Press, Inc.
A Sage Publications Company
2455 Teller Road
Thousand Oaks, California 91320
E-mail: order@corwinpress.com

SAGE Publications Ltd.
6 Bonhill Street
London EC2A 4PU
United Kingdom

SAGE Publications India Pvt. Ltd.
M-32 Market
Greater Kailash I
New Delhi 110 048 India

Printed in the United States of America

Library of Congress Cataloging-in-Publication Data

Osguthorpe, Russell T.
    Balancing the tensions of change: Eight keys to collaborative
educational renewal / by Russell T. Osguthorpe and Robert S.
Patterson.
        p. cm.
    Includes bibliographical references and index.
    ISBN 0-8039-6699-7 (cloth: acid-free paper)
    ISBN 0-8039-6700-4 (pbk.: acid-free paper)
    1. College-school cooperation. 2. Educational change. 3.
Interorganizational relations. I. Patterson, Robert S. II. Title.
    LB2331.53 .O74 1998
    378.1'03—ddc21   98-8902

This book is printed on acid-free paper.

98 99 00 01 02 03 10 9 8 7 6 5 4 3 2 1

Editorial Assistant: Julia Parnell
Production Editor: Diana E. Axelsen
Editorial Assistant: Denise Santoyo
Typesetter/Designer: Danielle Dillahunt
Cover Designer: Michelle Lee

Contents

Preface

When a person or group is attempting to improve any aspect of the human condition, questions always arise: Are we moving in the right direction? Will the change we are contemplating actually make things better? Doing something for the first time—even a seemingly minor modification of how things have been done in the past—involves risk. We view this book not only as an aid to those involved in the change process but as a risk-taking venture itself.

We have lived inside the longest-functioning partnership in the National Network for Educational Renewal, a consortium of 16 school-university partnerships organized by John I. Goodlad that extends from Maine to Hawaii (see Schlichtemeier, 1996). When John first came to Brigham Young University (BYU) in 1983 to explore the possibility of establishing such a partnership, similar organizations were rare in the nation. Now they are familiar to educators and state legislators not only in the United States but in many other countries.

Living through changes in our own partnership, and watching other collaborative organizations develop, we have seen both the possibilities and the pitfalls that partnerships offer. Just bringing people together to improve education is no guarantee of success. As we have worked through our own challenges and watched others face theirs, we have become convinced that anyone involved in collaborative change must continually examine the process as well as its outcomes. Otherwise groups disintegrate, and change is stifled.

We admit a bias in favor of working together rather than in isolation. This book is much different—better, we hope—than it would have been if either of us had tried to write it on our own. Although individual change will always be central to what we are discussing in this book, *collective* change is what is needed if schools—or any other organizations—are to make enduring improvements.

Tensions always accompany change. Sometimes these tensions arise from the fear one has of doing things differently. (How will this change affect me? Will I be able to do this?) Other times, the tensions arise from interpersonal differences. (How can you possibly see it that way? Are you implying that what I've been doing for the past 10 years is worthless?)

Rather than seeing such tensions as positive forces for change, many participants in collaborative work see them as insurmountable obstacles. When participants come to this negative view, they withdraw from the change process, and the collective improvements that we all seek in education are thwarted. Our purpose in writing this book is to help people involved in collaborative renewal come to see the inevitable tensions that arise as positive stimulants to change rather than as hindrances. Our observations of collaboratives in the United States and in other countries have demonstrated to us that viewing the tensions in positive ways can have dramatically beneficial effects on both people and programs.

Our hope is that this book will be useful to anyone involved in collaborative educational renewal: faculty and administrators in schools and universities, community leaders, parents, and students—particularly students preparing to be educators. Although the examples are drawn primarily from school-university collaboratives, we believe that anyone involved in interorganizational change could benefit from the ideas presented. The book is not limited to one stage of collaboration. Those who are just beginning to form collaborative organizations will benefit, but so will those whose partnerships are more mature. We believe that the book will be most beneficial if it is used as a discussion aid for groups of collaborators: for example, school principals and teachers meeting with university faculty and administrators. At whatever stage an interorganizational collaborative is functioning, this book will help participants examine both the process and the aims of their joint work.

Overview of the Book

In the introduction, we describe the challenges associated with the change process; define individual, institutional, and collaborative renewal; and identify eight tensions that emerge when unlike partners join together to work toward common goals.

Following the introduction, the book is organized in two parts: Part I, "Building Relationships of Mutuality," and Part II, "Crossing Thresholds to Creativity." In Part I, we show how forming proper relationships is prerequisite to renewal, and we describe the first three keys to balancing the tensions of change. Key 1 addresses the tensions associated with membership in the collaborative. On a national level, for example, organizers must determine which school-university consortia should be included in national networks; on a local level, governing boards must decide which schools should be considered as partner or professional development schools; and within a school or university, all individuals must decide to what degree they are members of the collaborative organization. This chapter describes principles for defining such membership and gives examples of membership criteria from functioning partnerships.

As educators come to see themselves as members of a school-university partnership, they begin to assume new professional roles. School educators may spend more of their time at the university, and university educators spend more of their time in the schools. Such cross-cultural experience leads to a tension between acting on the host group's perspective and maintaining individual identity. School educators might feel at times as if they are expected to behave like university educators, whereas university educators may feel pressure to behave like those in the schools. The chapter on Key 2 describes the type of role flexibility that is needed in collaborative change initiatives and includes suggestions for developing this type of flexibility among all participants.

For a partnership to endure, each partner must have a measure of altruism—a willingness to contribute freely to the group's goals. But members must also feel that collaborative efforts lead to the accomplishment of each partner's unique needs, a relationship we call *interdependence*. If either partner's needs are not met by the collective effort, the organization will eventually collapse, regardless of the degree of altruism that exists. While discussing Key 3, we treat the issues related to commitment and ways participants can achieve interdependence.

If roles are to be defined and commitment is to be developed, participants must actively work together to improve learning and teaching. Part II addresses the tensions and balance points associated with this type of creative work. Such collaborative initiatives might emerge in the form of highly structured, carefully planned programs, as spur-of-the-moment creative ideas, or as a healthy mix of structure and creativity. Drawing on actual projects that have been completed or are currently underway in school-university collaboratives, the chapter on Key 4 addresses issues associated with the planning that occurs in collaborative change initiatives.

Not only do participants need to achieve a balance between spontaneity and planning, they also must become inquiring change agents who express faith in one another's ability to succeed, yet questioning the efficacy of the work in which they are engaged. Establishing this kind of balance in school-university work is the topic of the chapter on Key 5.

Regardless of their approach to change, collaborators continually feel pressure to put into practice every good idea that emerges and an equally strong desire to perfect what is currently underway. Thus, some participants push to expand in every conceivable direction, whereas others want to reduce the size and number of initiatives to obtain greater focus. We call the balance between these two sides of the tension *disciplined openness*, a mindset that allows participants to consider a new idea while contemplating how the idea fits with current partnership work. In the chapter on Key 6, we address this tension and suggest ways to develop disciplined openness.

In discussing Key 7, we assert that traditional forms of evaluation are not adequate in a school-university partnership. A type of transformative evaluation is needed that draws on collaborative relationships. We have found that the tensions on either side of transformative evaluation—examining only the process or focusing exclusively on outcomes—can be positive forces for collecting valuable data, but that balance must be achieved if participants are to experience educational renewal.

We call the final tension *giving and receiving*. It is common in collaborative work for one partner to feel short-changed. For example, if teachers in partner schools believe that their contribution of time far exceeds that of the university faculty, and believe that the primary benefits of the teacher preparation program accrue to the university, they may press for uniformity of contribution, demanding that each partner spend an amount of time that correlates with the benefits received. In this case, the balance point of parity has not been achieved. A collaborative that has reached parity will be more interested in the benefits accruing to the children and youth in the classrooms than the relative size of each participant's contribution. This balance point depends on the preceding seven—only when the other tensions are in balance can parity be achieved.

In the final chapter, we summarize the points we make about each of the eight keys to collaborative educational renewal and offer additional metaphors that help encapsulate our approach to change.

Finally, the appendix lays the historical background for collaborative change in education. Although most educators have heard of normal schools, few understand the societal changes that have fueled the evolution from these institutions to the current schools of education and the emerging centers of pedagogy. In the appendix, we show how current centers of pedagogy are restoring some of the collaborative ties that once existed in normal and laboratory schools, and how these new relationships are essential to educational renewal.

We thank those who have assisted us in writing this book. We are grateful to the teachers and principals in our partner schools who have listened to our ideas and offered their suggestions. Our colleagues in the David O. McKay School of Education also offered valuable insights as we shared some of the contents of this book with them. We are particularly indebted to Sharon Black, not only for her competent editing but for her continuing willingness to share her transformative gifts.

About the Authors

Russell T. Osguthorpe is Associate Director of the Faculty Center and Professor of Pedagogy in the Center for the Improvement of Teacher Education and Schooling at Brigham Young University. He received his education at the University of Utah and BYU, receiving a PhD from BYU in Instructional Psychology. He has published widely in the areas of peer tutoring and the use of technology in special education, teacher education, and instructional science, and has served as a reviewer for the *Journal of Teacher Education* and the *Elementary School Journal.* He has directed funded projects in the United States and China and has served as a review panelist of grant applications for the U.S. Department of Education. He currently serves as a consultant to educational collaboratives in Québec and in Europe. He has been a visiting scholar at the University of Toronto and at the University of Paris, where he studied collaborative educational renewal in France.

Robert S. Patterson is Dean of the David O. McKay School of Education at Brigham Young University. Prior to joining BYU as Dean in 1992, he was Professor of Education at the University of Alberta in Edmonton, Alberta, Canada. During his 28 years at the University of

Alberta, he taught courses in the history of education. He also served as an administrator for 15 years, the last 8 as Dean of the Faculty of Education. He holds a master's degree from the University of Alberta and a PhD from Michigan State University in History and Philosophy of Education. In 1990, he was awarded an honorary Doctor of Letters by the University of Lethbridge. His writing and research are centered on the history of Canadian education, with focus on early 20th-century topics of normal school education, progressive education, and teacher education. He has authored numerous papers, book chapters, and articles and coedited three books or monographs. He also is a member of the governing board of the BYU-Public School Partnership.

Introduction

One of the great ironies of human behavior is that we often avoid doing the things that could save our lives. For example, most of us understand more of the benefits of good nutrition and exercise than we actually put into practice. One of the most compelling examples of this conflict between personal knowledge and behavior occurred in the search for a cure to the disease of scurvy. As early as 1628, it was reported that of those who arrived in America to found the town of Plymouth, fully half died of scurvy, but none of those who came on the next ship had the disease. And after the arrival of the second ship—"which brought store of juice of lemons—many recover[ed] speedily" (Carpenter, 1986, p. 12).

Even though sailors and the governments that supplied their ships knew that citrus fruits could prevent and cure scurvy, people were dying of the disease as late as three centuries after the "juice of lemons" was found to be beneficial. Some will assert that citrus fruits did not become a regular part of the food supply for sailors because medical professionals had not yet discovered vitamin C and shown its effects on the disease, but more likely is the explanation that humans are creatures of habit and have difficulty changing their behavior—in this case, their eating behavior.

Whether examining the change process as it applies to an individual's eating habits or to one's approach to learning and teaching, doing things differently is not easy for anyone. In fact, change seems to be a process that most of us value so long as we are not required to engage in it ourselves. Giving up a habit, a belief, or even an idea to which one has become attached can be an act of pain, an object of fear. As Dewey (1910) says, "Old ideas give way slowly; for they are more than abstract forms and categories. They are habits, predispositions, deeply ingrained attitudes of aversion and preference" (p. 19). Changing educational practice, as Dewey understood so well, is not a task for the faint of heart.

Facing change can be akin to confronting one's deepest fears, including death. When a person gives up a way of behaving, thinking, or feeling, that part of the person in one sense "dies" and is replaced with a new way of behaving, thinking, or feeling. Kenko, a 14th-century Japanese essayist, infers that change agents are much like soldiers going into battle:

> The soldier who goes to war, knowing how close he is to death, forgets his family and even forgets himself; the man who has turned his back on the world and lives in a thatched hut . . . may suppose that death in battle has nothing to do with him, but this is a shallow misconception. Does he imagine, that if he hides in the still recesses of the mountains, the enemy called change will fail to attack? When you confront death [change], no matter where it may be, it is the same as charging into battle. (quoted in Lopate, 1996, p. 31)

As Kenko asserts, to the soldier change is the enemy. But to the 17th-century sailors, change could have been their ultimate friend. Change itself is a paradox. It has the power to give life or to take it away. Knowing that change can make things either better or worse can cause anyone to fear the new and hold onto the familiar. This is why, as Dewey (1910) says, "old ideas give way slowly"—even ideas that have been proven harmful. One might wish for a world in which change would not confront everyone every day—a world that offers each of its inhabitants a way to escape into a "still recess in the mountains" (p. 19). But that is simply not the case.

When Jimmy Carter was asked in a television interview to describe the most important change he had experienced in his life, he responded without hesitation that it had been the advent of electricity. He told how the electric light had changed his life on the peanut farm, allowing him for the first time to do things after the sun went down. Viewers likely expected him to cite a change of law or a change in international relations, but he chose to mention the invention of electricity. This had been a "friendly" change for him, allowing him to read late into the evening (see Goldberg, 1991).

But even changes that first appear as friends can later seem like enemies. Electricity made it possible for factories to operate 24 hours each day, causing some people to work rotating shifts that have been shown to be physically and emotionally damaging. Electricity made it possible to create work-saving devices that have led to an unhealthy sedentary lifestyle. Now we're beginning as a culture to use electrical devices, such as treadmills, to help us get the physical exertion from which electricity was once supposed to have saved us.

Renewal

The word *renew* has been used in a variety of contexts. To renew something or someone can mean to "replace by some new or fresh thing," to "restore by fresh supply," to "refresh oneself," to "bring back into existence," to "make spiritually new or regenerate" (Simpson & Weinere, 1989, p. 613). In this book, we draw on all these meanings as we use the term *renewal* to express a kind of change that is at once both positive and enduring, a change that strengthens both individuals and institutions. Renewal is a continual process, a state of mind, a condition of the heart. Renewal has nothing to do with movements, reform initiatives, or restructuring projects. Each of these has beginning and ending points, whereas renewal—at least the way we are using it in this book—is a way of being that goes on and on.

Individual Renewal

Unlike some proponents of school change, we do not see educational renewal as a find-the-fault-and-fix-it process. Refreshing oneself has little to do with faults and much to do with nourishment and strengthening. Because education is at its core a human endeavor, technicistic approaches to change ultimately damage rather than help.

On a visit to a large computer firm, the first author was told by the director of training, "You may be interested in our new zero-defects program." Thinking that the program was aimed at producing more trouble-free computers, I nodded my head. Pointing to a diagram that covered all four walls in the room we were in, she responded, "We use this instructional design sequence in our training, and when someone misses a test item, we revisit the design, reteach the missed concept. If our instruction is as good as it should be, none of the trainees will be defective in their knowledge." I understood that she was not referring to computers as defective, or even to the instruction; rather, the firm labeled trainees themselves as defective when they missed items on the test.

Individual renewal is the antithesis of such technicistic orientation. Renewal means that educators experience things afresh, and by so doing are refreshed themselves. Learning—when it is not forced—can be a form of personal renewal. Students and teachers alike are changed by the learning they experience. They see things in new ways, understand differently, and as a result are able to do things that they could not do before. Personal renewal is a process of gaining strength day by day so that one can face the challenges that life brings.

Although this book emphasizes a form of renewal that occurs in groups, we recognize that groups are made up of individuals and that individual renewal is in one sense a prerequisite to institutional renewal. The poet, scientist, or artist who creates a new poem, theory, or painting is renewed in the process—and the act of creation is admittedly individual in nature. We applaud and encourage such individual effort. But even in isolation, a creative act usually affects more than the creator. The poem is read by others, the theory is tested, the painting is displayed. Thus, even individual renewal usually affects more than one person.

Institutional Renewal

If individuals are experiencing renewal, the institutions to which they belong will naturally be renewed as well. Ways of doing things will change to meet the needs of those the institution serves. Products will be modified and perfected, policies will be revised, and people will be cared for. But the idea of institutional renewal brings with it some unique challenges. An institution—be it a school, a hospital, or an automobile corporation—must respond to multiple audiences and constituencies, each of which has a vested interest in the institution. For example, educators may wish to make a significant change in their school, but parents may not support the proposal. The automobile corporation may make a change at headquarters that its dealers do not support.

Partly because of the complexities of institutional change, some have argued that the only type of change that is possible is individual. To a point, they are right. The changes that occur in the "inward person" are those that matter most. Most people have seen mandated change that was later undone by individuals who did not support it. But we maintain in this book that anyone interested in making things better—whether it be in schools or in any other part of our society— must eventually come to grips with institutional or group change. And such change, if it is effective, has the potential to renew all associated with the institution.

Collaborative Renewal

Although both individual and institutional renewal are essential in a healthy society, they are not enough. Another type of renewal occurs across and between institutions. We call this type of change process *collaborative renewal*. This is a type of renewal that occurs between unlike partners—people who have at least one common goal, but who have other goals that differ. In its simplest form, the family fits our definition. Each member of the family has a goal to help the others, but one may be pursuing a college degree while another is working full time. The knowledge and skills of family members might differ considerably, but all members are committed to each other in ways that cause them at times to make sacrifices for the common good.

In more complex forms, interinstitutional or collaborative re-newal might cause business leaders, church officials, and educators to work with law enforcement agencies to curb violence in their city. The power of such four-way collaboration comes from the common goal that all partners share, but it also comes from the varied skills and knowledge that the different participants can bring to the initia-tive. This variance in background can lead to a more effective achievement of the common goal, but it can also lead to personal and institutional renewal for all involved. When the law enforcement officer begins to see the problem from the viewpoint of the educator, or when the business leader sees the problem through the eyes of the church official, all are somehow changed in the process: All are made stronger in addressing the common goal.

Our premise is that collaborative educational renewal is not only desirable but necessary if our society is to survive. Just as British sailors were slow to accept the fact that citrus fruits would heal their scurvy, our society is slow to recognize the necessity of working together for the betterment of education. Although some desire to let the schools fend for themselves, others are beginning to realize that the schools cannot educate the citizenry single-handed. There must be a community-wide effort to educate the young to live in a democracy. John Goodlad (1997) says:

> Equally important and recently more neglected is attention to collective democratic character—to the making of civil communities. Caring, interpersonal symbiotics are a necessary part of such but not sufficient. There must be a civic cultural conscience. The contrast between ideal and reality is great.

Quoting Stephen Gould, Goodlad continues:

> Our culture does not nourish that which is best or noblest in the human spirit. It does not cultivate vision, imagination, or aesthetic or spiritual sensitivity. It does not encourage gentleness, generosity, caring, or compassion. Increasingly in the late 20th century, the economic-technocratic-static worldview has become a monstrous destroyer of what is loving and life-affirming in the human soul. (p. 124)

The "civic cultural conscience" that Goodlad (1997) speaks of, and the "life-affirming" qualities that Gould is calling for are inherent in our definition of collaborative renewal. Whether the cooperation extends across one's street to a neighbor or across the ocean to one's international business partner, our form of democracy will demand ever greater levels of collaborative renewal. The tasks of the next millennium will require more sharing of expertise, more selfless giving. For such sharing and giving to occur, all will need to come to a better understanding of what it means to truly collaborate.

Tensions of Change

Any time unlike partners come together, tensions arise. Because each partner sees things differently, each imagines different solutions to a common problem. This is at once the opportunity and the risk associated with collaborative renewal. Although tensions can emerge in individual creative work, interpersonal tensions are substantively different and more complex. Even in the classroom, tensions are present. The teacher's and students' expectations can "pull" on one another. If the tug is too strong, frustration can arise, and learning can cease.

Like classroom renewal—in which teachers and learners are experiencing change—collaborative renewal brings with it certain tensions. We have identified eight such tensions from our own experience in partnership work and from our observation and study of others' similar efforts. Though each tension may be viewed as distinct, we have grouped them into two main poles that we designate too subjective and too objective (see Table 1). These poles represent fundamental human needs: the subjective, the need to contribute something new, to be supportive of others, or "let things go," and the objective, the need to adhere to cultural tradition, to prove the worth of one's work, and to live by the rules by which institutions and citizens are governed (Patterson & Osguthorpe, 1996).

Although both of these needs are necessary to the change process, there is danger in moving too far to either side—relying too much on unrestrained spontaneity (subjectivity) or too much on controlled planning (objectivity). Interpersonal relationships remain at the base of the change process. For a partnership to balance the subjective and objective poles, participants must develop relationships that lead to improvements in teaching and learning.

We might compare a collaborative organization to a suspension bridge that has eight main anchor points (the tensions), each with a steel tower (balance), and with steel cable on either side of each tower (the two poles of the eight positive tensions). When each of the cables is equally taut, the support poles remain vertical (balanced), and the bridge stays upright and secure. But if any cable loses its tension

TABLE 1. Tensions, Poles, and Keys Associated with Collaborative Educational Renewal

Tension	Too Subjective	Balanced	Too Objective
Membership	*Motivation:* Membership is based primarily on individual desire to participate.	*Informed membership:* Participation is based on the interests, abilities, and needs of each partner.	*Performance:* Membership is based primarily on individual and institutional performance.
Roles	*Group perspective:* Participants relinquish their traditional roles and lose their institutional identity.	*Role flexibility:* Partners shift roles as needed while retaining institutional identity.	*Individual identity:* Participants hold to their traditional roles and their institutional identity.
Commitment	*Altruism:* Participants work solely to meet their partner's needs.	*Interdependence:* Participants work to meet their partner's and their own needs simultaneously.	*Self-interest:* Participants work solely to meet their own needs.
Planning	*Spontaneous renewal:* Emphasis is placed on unplanned change.	*Nurtured development:* Partners sustain both planned and unplanned initiatives of mutual benefit.	*Planned change:* Emphasis is placed on goal-setting and strategic planning.
Approach to Change	*Champion:* Change initiatives of limited worth succeed because some participants champion the cause.	*Inquiring change agentry:* Participants support each other in thoughtful examination of each change initiative.	*Critic:* Worthy change initiatives fail because some participants offer excessive criticism.

through neglect, excessive stress, or environmental effects, the bridge loses its power to support those who wish to travel across it. And if

TABLE 1. *Continued*

Tension	Too Subjective	Balanced	Too Objective
Amount of Change	*Expansion:* New change initiatives are embraced without regard for partnership-wide effect.	*Disciplined openness:* New change initiatives are considered in light of current work.	*Focus:* Current change initiatives drive partnership work and exclude new proposals from consideration.
Evaluation	*Process evaluation:* Partners justify their work based on the quality of partnership relationships and activities.	*Transformative evaluation:* Partners jointly reach their common goals by freely sharing observations and data.	*Outcome evaluation:* Partners demand objective evidence to justify each partnership initiative.
Giving and Receiving	*Diversity:* Partners make varying contributions and receive different benefits without regard for equity.	*Parity:* Participants give and receive with equity, thought, and grace.	*Uniformity:* Partners must contribute the same resources and receive the same benefits.

multiple cables are too tight or too loose, the towers begin to tilt, losing their ability to suspend the main beam, and the bridge collapses. Using the metaphor of the bridge, Figure 1 illustrates the positive tensions of school-university partnerships.

Although any tension can arise in collaborative work at any time, we believe that leaders of collaborative organizations should focus on each tension sequentially. In other words, building proper relationships (Part I) must occur before engaging in creative change (Part II). And qualifications for membership (the first tension) should be resolved before roles for participants are defined. As collaborative work unfolds, these tensions may reappear, but if they are balanced in the early stages, they will need much less attention later, and the collaborative renewal will have a much greater chance of success.

Figure 1. Keys to Collaborative Educational Renewal

By defining the eight tensions and focusing on the processes of collaboration, we are not inferring that change occurs only in groups or that leaders should stop thinking about the needs of individuals. We support the caution of Fullan and Hargreaves (1996) that collaboration not be viewed by educators as an end in itself. Change comes one person at a time, and schools and universities would do well to increase their emphasis on the development of individual faculty. Institutional or societal development—the kind of change we seek in a democracy—comes only when people work together to achieve a common goal, only when they develop what we call "relationships of mutuality."

PART ONE

Building Relationships of Mutuality

Every real relation with a being or life in the world is exclusive. Its Thou is freed, steps forth, is single, and confronts you. It fills the heavens. This does not mean that nothing else exists; but all else lives in its light.

—Martin Buber, *I and Thou*

While conducting a tour of a newly established partner school located in a large urban center, the assistant principal fielded questions from the group. After observing a 5th-grade classroom, one visitor asked, "Could you please explain the roles of the two teachers we just saw?" The guide eagerly responded, "We call the one who was speaking a 'mentor teacher,' and the one who was working with students at their seats a 'visiting teacher.'" Following a description of each teacher's role, an education professor from the school's partner university asked the guide to discuss the learning resource center the group had just passed. The guide's pleasant demeanor immediately changed, and with a "you-should-know-better" look in her eye, snapped back, "I am not taking any questions from university people right now." At that point, the professor ushered a

1

few of us into the learning resource center and explained how the center had been a source of contention between school and university participants.

We had observed such contention in our own partnership and were not surprised to find it in this partner school. Whenever people with different roles and backgrounds come together, friction is likely to occur—largely because participants do not yet understand each other. The guide apparently interpreted the professor's intervention as an attack on the credibility of the partner school's leaders, whereas the professor seemed only to be seeking an answer to her question. Their interaction indicated that not everyone in the partnership had learned to trust one another; in Donna Kerr's (1997) terms, they had not yet established "relationships of mutuality" (p. 78).

Mutuality and Collaboration

Drawing on the philosophy of Martin Buber, Kerr (1997) explains that relationships of mutuality can be attained only when "one neither dominate[s] nor [is] subservient to another, neither use[s] another nor [is] used by another" (p. 78). On the surface, these "thou shalt nots" sound rather simple, even easy. But relating to others without imposing our will on them—as shown by the interaction between the school administrator and the university professor—demands that we place the other person's needs before our own. It requires that we engage in what Berry (1985) calls "genuine dialogue"—that we "open [ourselves] to the risk, the danger, and the surprise that go with dialogue, [and that we] let genuine dialogue unfold as it may" (p. 94). To open oneself to genuine dialogue and to be unwilling to dominate or to use another person requires that humans avoid their naturally self-centered tendencies—something that is neither simple nor easy.

It has been commented that "collaboration is an unnatural act among consenting adults" (J. I. Goodlad, personal communication, August 8, 1997). Rather than competing with or ignoring one another, collaborators work jointly on a common goal. They recognize that neither one could accomplish alone what they can achieve together. To develop communities characterized by collaboration, participants must recognize their common interests, come to agreement about the roles each will play, and then work for the realization of their shared aims. Such work demands that participants understand each other and come to value one another's goals—that they "have the real things of their common life in common; where they can experience, discuss and administer them together" (Buber, 1950, p. 15).

When we speak of collaboration in this book, we are not including all types of joint effort. If parties only share information, keep track of each other's activities, or periodically consult with one another, they are not engaging in the kind of collaboration necessary for educational or organizational renewal. Even archenemies share certain types of information, predict each other's next moves, and meet from time to time to negotiate their differences. These types of encounters are clearly not based on the kind of genuine dialogue that Berry (1985) claims is essential for relationships of mutuality to develop.

The joint effort required to engage in collaborative educational renewal includes two primary elements: 1) relationships of mutuality, and 2) agreement to pursue common goals. When either of these elements is missing or weak, personal and organizational renewal will diminish. These two elements are not only prerequisites to the process of renewal but are themselves personally (and hence organizationally) renewing. Successful collaboration cannot occur unless parties treat each other as equals without attempting to control or manipulate one another. As such mutuality develops, each participant becomes more creative, more able to take risks, and more willing to devote effort to a common agenda for change. Thus, relationships among participants and the agreements between partners must be constantly reassessed as renewal unfolds.

Indicators of Mutuality

Although genuine dialogue is an essential element of collaborative educational renewal, four other indicators characterize relationships of mutuality: 1) interest, 2) commitment, 3) caring, and 4) involvement. Those engaged in the change process could benefit by determining the degree to which each indicator is present in their own collaborative work.

Interest

Every experienced teacher recognizes the importance of personal desires and interests in learning and teaching. Horace Mann once said that "a teacher who is attempting to teach without inspiring the pupil with a desire to learn is hammering on cold iron" (cited in Paris & Ayres, 1994, p. 25). The desire to learn is based on the student's interests at the moment. In a classroom, unless the interests of both student and teacher merge, maximum learning will not occur (see Renninger, Hidi, & Krapp, 1992). So it is with collaborative change in education: Partners must first identify their common interests, otherwise they will be unable to create a community where participants learn from one another, the kind of community that fosters continual renewal.

When journalists design a layout for the front page of the newspaper, or television producers select a certain program for a given time slot, they are basing their decisions at least partially on general *human interest*—what will attract the public to read or view the selection. Although many people may be interested in a certain topic or story, these are not the type of interests that necessarily lead to relationships of mutuality or organizational change. They are what some have called "like interests," as opposed to "common interests" (see Clark, 1996, p. 35). Like interests are those we just happen to share with others—many of whom we may not know or ever meet. For example, many might share an interest in gardening, classical music, or antique automobiles. When a group of people comes together "to pursue one single comprehensive interest of them all," such as the improvement of learning and teaching in a given school, "we may call that interest a *common interest*" (MacIver, 1924, p. 103).

Commitment

As members of a community find a common interest and begin working on it, they become committed to achieving a particular goal. Our community recently became interested in preserving a century-old building by transforming it into a city library. Interest in the project grew slowly over several years as donors one by one offered their resources. But the entire community eventually had to make its will known by voting for or against a proposed property tax increase that would provide the remaining resources needed to complete the restoration of the aging building. Because the members of the community were generally well-informed, and because they had developed a common interest, the tax provision succeeded and the contracts were let to commence construction. Not until the common interest had evolved into a real commitment were citizens ready to "invest" in the restoration.

Any change process requires the development of such commitment. When community members join together to renew a school, the outside structure of the building may not change in any noticeable way, but the teaching and learning practices that occur inside its walls can be altered significantly. These changes require that members of the educational community find their common interest and allow that interest to develop into commitment, just as was necessary to transform a decaying building into a city library. But the level of interest and commitment needed to renew schools is much greater than that demanded to restore a building. Collaborative renewal calls community members to a higher form of personal action than simply voting for a tax increase: It asks for their creative contribution, for their thought, and for their affection.

Caring

Although educators must find a common interest and develop a shared commitment to improve learning, collaborative renewal will not succeed unless participants *care* for one another. Relationships of mutuality must be fostered among all members of the collaborative: teachers, administrators, students, parents, and community members. The hallmark of relationships of mutuality is caring. As Nel Noddings (1992) explains:

> The desire to be cared for is almost certainly a universal human characteristic. Not everyone wants to be cuddled and fussed over. But everyone wants to be received, to elicit a response that is congruent with an underlying need or desire. When we understand that everyone wants to be cared for and that there is no recipe for caring, we see how important attention is. In order to respond as a genuine carer, one does have to empty the soul of its contents. One cannot say, "Aha! This fellow needs care. Now, let's see—here are the seven steps I must follow." Caring is a way of being in relation, not a set of specific behaviors. (p. 17)

Caring cannot be mandated by a principal or superintendent; it must grow out of common interest and commitment naturally. Rogers (1994) describes how caring developed in an urban 4th-grade classroom, and Van Galen (1996) discusses her observations of caring in a Catholic high school. In both cases, observers perceived teachers themselves as the initiators of caring learning environments—not out of a response to administrative edict, but because this was these teachers' "way of being in relation."

For collaborative educational renewal to occur, all participants must be eager to *give* and *receive* caring. Students need to care for teachers, as well as teachers for students, and those who are pursuing educational change projects together (parents, educators, community leaders, students) must care for one another. Otherwise the effort expended in new initiatives will be in vain. The terms *buy into* and *ownership* are used frequently by those engaged in the change process: for example, "Until we get the teachers (university, or parents) to buy into our idea, we're dead in the water." These terms often imply that it is the job of some leader to "sell" an idea to other potential participants. The type of common interest, commitment, and caring that we are discussing has little to do with buying into or owning ideas. The kind of caring inherent in relationships of mutuality causes participants to focus on one another rather than on propositions imposed from some external source. The ideas that give rise to collaborative renewal projects grow out of the needs expressed by individuals in the collaborative, and the focus remains fixed on meeting those needs—the care always directed toward individuals rather than toward some abstract goal.

Involvement

If a person genuinely cares for another, positive action is inevitable. Even a passerby who needs directions elicits a helpful response if we care about the person. But the care that is required in collaborative educational renewal is substantively different from that of helping the passerby. Relationships of mutuality are formed over an extended period of time during which each partner voluntarily responds to the other's needs. At times, one partner gives while the other receives, and then the tables turn and the giver becomes the receiver. As the involvement of partners increases, the collaborative comes closer to the realization of the goals that grew out of the initial common interest that drew the partners together. The nature of the involvement thus becomes the key barometer of the health of the relationship and the effectiveness of the collaborative.

Any group engaged in joint effort to achieve a common goal might pose the following questions about the types of involvement members of the group are experiencing: a) To what degree is participation voluntary? b) Have participants found a balance between giving and receiving? c) What evidence is there that participants care for one another? d) Are all collaborative activities focused on the common goal? If the conditions in these questions are met—if participation is indeed voluntary, participants give and receive, care for one another, and focus continually on the common goal that brought them together, involvement will be healthy, and collaborative education renewal will thrive. If, however, participation is mandated, some participants always give while others receive, the members do not care for another, as participants lose their original focus, the collaborative work will diminish and renewal will fail.

Metaphors for Mutuality

Every collaborative endeavor differs in important ways, but in some ways all are similar. Metaphors help us capture these similarities and differences and communicate them to those within the group, as well as to those who are considering joining (see Stewart, 1997). Not only do metaphors help us describe what is going on in collaborative work, they are also an essential ingredient in the effective leadership of any organization (see Illes, 1997).

Family

Discussing their participation in Jackson Elementary School, Lynn Beck and Joseph Murphy (1996) use the word *family* to describe the kind of learning community they saw developing:

> Often it seemed to us that site council decision-making sessions were like those families might have, with persons sitting somewhat haphazardly around (and even on) tables, engaging in easy and candid conversation in the absence of formal "Robert's Rules of Order"-type procedures. Interactions between teachers— especially those between veterans and novices—seemed so natural that they too caused us to think of the help siblings or parents and children might offer to each other. (pp. 87-88)

The family metaphor captures the four characteristics of relationships of mutuality. Healthy families have common interests (beliefs, values, even mission statements; Covey, 1997), are committed to each other, care for one another, and actively contribute to each other's well-being. Such families accomplish important things together and take joy in each other's successes—precisely the kind of involvement that is at the heart of collaborative educational renewal. The metaphor, however, also has its downside.

For some, the word *family* brings to mind more than positive scenes of parents and children gathered around a dinner table in uplifting conversation. Robert Bly (1996) reminds that in current American culture "adults regress toward adolescence; and adolescents—seeing that—have no desire to become adults. Few are able to imagine any genuine life coming from the vertical plane—tradition, religion, devotion" (p. viii). The respect and care that were once integral to family life have faded, leaving children and parents who are more concerned about their own needs than the needs of each other.

The richness of the images that *family* evokes—both negative and positive—makes the metaphor a powerful lens through which collaborative work can be viewed. Participants in a collaborative project might characterize their work together as that of a healthy family in which each person cares equally for all others—as they did in Jackson Elementary School. But if discussion takes on a more selfish tone of "why me?" participants can use the image of warring siblings to restore mutuality and bring back the kind of genuine dialogue that will allow them to achieve the common goal—just as families can solve their differences by counseling together.

Team

The team metaphor is often used by collaborators to describe the way participants work together. Those on a team have specific roles because of their individual talents and training. For example, the first author's daughter Lisa plays guard-forward on her high school basketball team. The point guard on her team is several inches shorter than Lisa, whereas the center is several inches taller. Each player is uniquely suited to make a specific contribution to the team—the point guard brings the ball down the court and sets up the offense, whereas the center stays close to the basket ready to score. Prior to her senior year, Lisa played on a state all-star team that played other teams throughout the nation. The purpose of these exhibition games was to permit college coaches to select high school players they wished to recruit for their teams.

While watching the exhibition games, I could easily distinguish differences between the all-stars and Lisa's high school team. The all-star teams were collections of talented players who each wanted to "show what she could do," whereas the regular high school team played with a clear common goal in mind: winning. The all-stars seemed much less concerned about winning than they were about meeting their own individual goals to be recruited. Each of the players played well, and the team was moderately successful, but the team spirit was not at all what it had been on the high school team.

The team metaphor is apt for relationships of mutuality. Educators who collaborate are often like the all-star team members: They do not know each other very well, they are not well-informed about each member's talents and skills, and each engages in collaborative work solely for his or her own benefit. When collaborative educational renewal takes place, however, participants become well acquainted, assume roles that uniquely fit their abilities, and work with the common goal in mind. Just as a family can experience difficult times, a team might encounter periods of turmoil when certain team members cannot get along, or when there is fundamental disagreement about how play should proceed. Again, the team metaphor can be useful to those attempting to develop relationships of mutuality because they can use the metaphor to explain temporary problems and create possible solutions.

Symbiosis

Symbiosis is a biological term referring to "the living together of two dissimilar organisms, especially when this association is mutually beneficial" (Stein & Urdang, 1983, p. 1440). John Goodlad (1994) often uses the metaphor of symbiosis to describe school-university partnerships. He suggests that effective symbiotic relationships between two organizations, such as a K-12 school and a university, have four primary characteristics:

1) distinctive differences between the courting parties, 2) the complementarity of these differences—the degree to which each side

contributes to the other's lack, 3) the degree to which this complementarity depends on commitment and effort fully shared,
and 4) powerful contextual contingencies (pp. 104-105)

Just as members of a family or a team differ in abilities and
interests, symbiotic partners are distinct from one another. They
retain their own identity even when they find themselves on the
other's turf. And, as with all relationships of mutuality, such partners
meet each other's needs by committing themselves and becoming
involved in a shared agenda.

Stages of Mutuality

Relationships of mutuality develop in stages. Each time a new participant is invited to collaborate, the person will progress from one
of the earlier stages before developing lasting trust. Some new participants are largely uninformed about the purposes of the collaborative and therefore ignore it. They are unable to articulate the
common interest of the group, for example, "I never have been able
to understand what the partnership is all about." Some might enter
at a point when they can describe the common interest, but they
doubt the sincerity or authenticity of the other participants, for
example, "It seems to me that this is an organization on paper only.
I challenge anyone to show me what it has done to help kids."
    Other participants might enter the collaborative able to describe
its purposes and eager to contribute, but they have not yet become
acquainted with the work of the organization and know few people
in it, for example, "I learned today at a meeting that the partnership
is emphasizing literacy in all the partner schools." Some understand
the joint effort, value it, are acquainted with other participants, and
are eager to accept a role in the collaborative work: "I think I could
contribute by finding instruments that we could all agree measure a
child's ability to read." The final stage often requires more time than
any of the preceding ones. Trust usually develops in small, often
imperceptible increments: "We could accomplish something important together."
    The early stages of building relationships of mutuality are "I"
centered, whereas the final stage of trust is "we" centered—the kind
of trust that is essential in relationships of mutuality, the kind of trust

required for renewal. In a widely publicized attempt to reform public education during the past decade, educational leaders in Rochester, New York, invited a wide array of community participants to join with them to improve their inner-city schools. To involve the business community, the educators invited Kay Whitmore, president of Eastman Kodak, the largest single employer in the city. In describing how he gradually developed trust in the reform effort, Whitmore said, "In the past, when I saw a superintendent at a dinner, we would chat mostly about the weather or sports. [Now we] talk about education" (Buckley, 1989, p. 59).

When a group of young business leaders in Rochester came together for a pep talk on working together to improve public education, Whitmore, who had already been collaborating with educators for some time cautioned, "Be prepared to work very hard for a long time. The more time I spend on [school reform], the more complicated it gets" (Buckley, 1989, p. 58). Whitmore admitted that as a leader of a *Fortune* 500 company, he was not very well-informed about how to conduct K-12 schooling. Although he had experienced the schools himself and had watched his own children experience them, he had never been asked to assist with a concerted effort to improve schooling.

As he became more involved in the collaborative work of reform, however, he became acquainted with the other collaborators, came to accept the common goals of the reform effort, and developed trust in the educators with whom he was working. His injunction to the new initiates was sobering. He was trying to help them understand that although they might be accustomed to quick fixes in their business, they should not expect to see schools change overnight. We believe that one of the reasons for his cautions grew out of the realization that schools are complex organizations, and that to help them improve requires a level of mutual trust rarely seen in organizational change efforts.

Mutuality and
Collaborative Renewal

Any organization that wishes to renew itself by collaborating with partners outside its normal boundaries must answer three questions dealing with relationships: 1) Who may belong? 2) What is required of those who join? and 3) What's in it for me? Each of these questions focuses on one of the tensions that arise in collaborative renewal, tensions that must be kept in balance if the collaborative effort is to succeed. When balance is achieved for each of the three tensions, relationships of mutuality will be a dominant feature of the organization. When balance on any one of the tensions is lost, relationships will suffer and common goals will not be achieved.

Relationships are thus the first key, the foundation of all we do to improve the educational experience of those who come within our stewardship. When our relationships are strong, meaningful, and mutually enriching, our work as educators thrives, and we experience the same kind of renewal that we are attempting to impart to our students. But when we are not in harmony with those around us—when we resent a colleague for any reason—our ability to nurture others is hampered, and the possibilities for renewal evaporate. As Lowell L. Bennion, a lifelong educator, said,

> We live and move and have our being in each other as well as in God. The most important thing in life is the quality of our human relationships, not only in the intimate family circle and friendship circle, but in relationships with all [others]. (quoted in England, 1988, p. 26)

Key #1

Qualified Membership

When we met with the dean of education at Hebrew University, we discussed the idea of school-university partnerships. At one point in the conversation, the dean, looking puzzled, leaned forward in his chair and asked,

> I have thought about establishing such partnerships. But how do you decide which school districts to include? It seems to me that every district wants to join with us, but I'm afraid that if we spread ourselves so thinly, we won't be able to accomplish anything of real worth. And I worry that all of these schools are thinking more about the benefits they will receive from the partnership than they are about the contributions they will make.

The dean was asking what every interested leader of collaborative renewal must ask: Who should belong? Not wanting to disappoint or alienate principals or superintendents who had expressed interest in joining the partnership, he was reluctant to say no to some and yes to others. What basis would he use for including some and excluding others? Would he be able to identify a defensible set of criteria that could be used to make membership decisions without damaging the relationships he already enjoyed with the K-12 educators? With these criteria, would he be able to limit the number of participants to a manageable number? As this example shows, the questions related to membership develop into a tension even before collaborative work begins.

Qualifying for Membership

When John Goodlad and his associates organized the current version of the National Network for Educational Renewal (NNER), they first needed to articulate how an interested institution would qualify for membership in the network. Of the approximately 250 institutions that expressed initial interest, 16 were eventually selected based on the degree to which each was prepared to pursue a common agenda articulated in 19 postulates aimed at the simultaneous improvement of schooling and teacher education.

To be considered for membership, each institution submitted a proposal describing the nature of the institution's school-university partnership and discussing the partnership's performing on each of the 19 postulates. The heart of the proposal was a description of how the partnership planned to meet the criteria for each of the postulates in the future.

Postulate 17, for example, states that teacher education programs "must establish linkages with graduates for purposes of both evaluating and revising the programs and easing the critical early years of transition into teaching" (Goodlad, 1994, p. 91). Because our institution sends its graduates to all 50 states and beyond, we felt particularly vulnerable on this postulate. Procedures for following up with our graduates were not nearly as effective as they needed to be. In writing the proposal to join NNER, however, we described a method for establishing better linkages with graduates, especially with those in our partner schools.

The process for joining NNER blended the two poles of the membership tension shown in Figure 1 on p. xxii of this volume. Each partnership that applied was required to describe the degree to which it was attending to the common interest (the postulates), as well as explain its desires to improve. Individual and organizational motivation for change was as important as institutional *perfor-*

mance related to the postulates. By requiring institutions to determine their own commitment to the common interest—by both performance and motivation, Goodlad had found a way to balance the tension related to membership.

But membership in collaborative work occurs at two levels: institutional and individual. Simply because a school-university partnership is selected as a member of NNER does not necessarily mean that each individual in the partner institutions is equally committed to the prospect of collaborative renewal. Such commitment becomes particularly apparent when a principal and teachers are deciding whether or not to submit an application to become a partner school. When faced with such a decision, individual teachers have decided to transfer to another school rather than take on the responsibilities of teachers in a partner school. The key is *qualifications*: Whether building a national network of institutions or identifying partner schools within a single partnership, collaborators must agree on the standards of performance and the types of motivation necessary for participation.

Balancing the Tensions

If no one can qualify for membership in an organization, the organization cannot be established, and if everyone qualifies—regardless of behavior or motives—the organization has no reason to exist. The tensions that surround membership are thus positive forces that constantly cause leaders to reassess the organization's accomplishments and its future direction. Churches, businesses, schools, and universities must all decide what constitutes membership in their organization and the process for qualifying for such membership. Even public schools that were created to be maximally inclusive deny some children entry if they are too young, too old, or live outside certain boundaries. At times, these same schools discontinue the membership of teachers or students who were formerly admitted—often because of behavior that does not comply with accepted standards.

Although established organizations typically have a well-developed set of standards for admission and continued participation, hybrid organizations, such as school-university partnerships, often have poorly developed standards. These organizations might assume that the standards already in place in their individual institutions will be adequate for the newly formed collaborative. But because the partnership itself is a different organization, participants must come to agreement about qualifications for membership. For example, if a partner school agrees to engage in a fourfold mission of 1) educator preparation, 2) professional development, 3) curriculum development, and 4) research and inquiry, collaborators should continually determine the degree to which the school is, in fact, engaged in each of the four missions (see Osguthorpe, Harris, Harris, & Black, 1994). When teachers in a partner school collectively determine that they no longer want to mentor student teachers, they are deciding to give up their status as a partner school. Their membership in the organization has changed.

Identifying Common Interests

To determine qualifications for membership, unlike partners must first identify common interests—the same initial ingredient in relationships of mutuality. This process must remain at the base of all partnership activity, and thus as the central criterion for membership in the collaborative organization. When our partnership was formed, John Goodlad met separately with university personnel and with district superintendents to identify common interests. In Goodlad's (1994) words:

> To BYU personnel, I posed the question, "What might you have to gain from a close partnership with the schools? About a dozen major areas of potential benefit emerged. On Wednesday at a meeting on their turf, I asked the five superintendents the same question. Again, about a dozen major topics emerged. There was overlap in about half of the topics agreed upon by each group. On Thursday of that week, on the neutral turf of the hotel, I presented six topics identified commonly by the two groups as a possible agenda for collaboration. With incredible speed and unanimity, the combined groups agreed to form a school-university partnership to address this agenda of overlapping self-interests. (p. 107)

During these introductory meetings, those considering forming a hybrid organization were in reality defining the requirements for membership. The overlapping self-interests eventually became the previously mentioned fourfold mission of partner schools. In essence, universities needed places to conduct educational research (inquiry) and provide student teachers with practical experience (educator preparation), and schools needed ways of improving teaching practice (professional development) and enhancing K-12 instruction (curriculum development). Although superintendents and deans were not thinking in these terms at the time, they were saying in essence, "If you want to be in our partnership, you need to agree to contribute to these four common interests."

Developing the Invitation List

When one senses a need to join with others to accomplish a task, it is not necessary to invite everyone. Some collaborative efforts fail simply because of their unwieldy size. If participants cannot communicate easily—and some of this communication must be face to face—the newly formed organization will likely fail. Limiting the invitation list to those who show genuine interest is essential in collaborative educational renewal. When our partnership was formed, we could have invited all 40 districts in the state to participate, but we chose instead to invite only 5.

To develop a list of potential collaborators, one should do the following:

- Assess interests.
- Estimate commitment.
- Imagine roles.
- Take risks.

Because collaborative work usually grows out of some looser form of cooperation, most potential invitees are already known to the one who is considering a more formal relationship. Our university, for example, had been sending student teachers to the five school districts for many years before we established our school-university partnership. We could quite easily predict those who might be interested in working with us. We understood something about the possibilities and limitations of their organizations, as they did ours.

In fact, like most schools and universities, we regularly complained about each other's institutions. Although those in the schools and the university realized that each institution was somewhat dependent on the other for its own existence, representatives from each sector had never discussed at length how closer collaboration might be mutually beneficial. We had never assessed the interests of our potential partner. In one sense, we had courted but never married.

Interests might be assessed through conversation with potential participants, but *commitment* implies action. Because our partnership was in the early stages of development, we invited those who had already evidenced their commitment by the ways that they had contributed to our common goals—particularly in the area of mentoring student teachers. Schools that had been particularly effective in this regard were some of the earliest candidates to become partner schools.

Any organization that is emerging should imagine the various roles that individuals will play once they are given participant responsibility. We use the word *imagine* because collaborative work worthy of its name always changes participants' roles to some degree. A 4th-grade teacher who is accustomed to worrying about her children takes on the role of student teacher mentor and begins to worry as well about the college student in her classroom. The university faculty member who usually focuses on the needs of her college students becomes involved in the instruction of fourth graders while collaborating inside the school.

Those inviting potential collaborators often overlook the importance of imagining roles before people are invited to participate. If, for example, a school-university partnership is deciding to emphasize collaborative research and inquiry, individuals must be invited into the new organization who have the skills and commitment to accomplish this task. In the beginning years of our partnership, we invited many who had interests and commitment related to teacher education but few who had experience with collaborative inquiry. Administrators, deans, teachers, and university faculty had all agreed that research was a central interest, but it kept getting short-changed— largely because partnership leaders did not invite participants who could have contributed in this way. This contrasts sharply with the kind of joint work that Jean Clandinin and others have developed at the University of Alberta (see Clandinin, Davies, Hogan, & Kennard, 1993), or the work of Helen Stewart at the Brock Centre for Collaborative Research (see Stewart, 1993). In both of these cases, collaborative inquiry was at the heart of the enterprise when the initial participants were invited to join.

Risk taking is an important ingredient to any change process, but it should not be overlooked in the beginning stage of forming the organization. Some risk is necessary even when extending invitations to potential participants. One can devote serious effort to assessing interest, estimating commitment, and imagining roles, and still fail to invite some who might be the strongest contributors to the collaborative endeavor. Not until our partnership was into its second decade did we consider inviting the state superintendent of public instruction to participate with us. Now he serves as a member of our partnership governing board, contributing not only his ideas but also resources needed to accomplish partnership goals.

Reviewing Membership

Balancing the tensions surrounding membership continues long after participants have accepted an invitation to collaborate on a common interest. Placing too much emphasis on either performance or motivation can destroy an organization. If, for example, participants are contributing their time solely out of obligation to an institutional mandate, the quality of the work will diminish, and the collaborative effort will fail. Similarly, if participants are highly motivated but do not possess the skills or background that allow them to contribute to the collaborative project, the change process will eventually disintegrate. Thus, even after people have begun to work together, the questions of performance and motivation remain essential to the success of the renewal process. Although a participant might eagerly accept an invitation to collaborate, personal and professional factors may change, reducing the effectiveness of the person's contribution. The four following principles will help keep the membership tension in balance as renewal efforts unfold:

- Participation need not be all or nothing.
- Collaborative work is not eternal.
- The exit door should be lighted and open.
- Leaving can be temporary.

Those who participate in collaborative educational renewal are often made to feel that they must give more time than they can possibly give—that renewal is an all-or-nothing venture. As a project draws on, some feel overburdened because they believe that they are carrying an unfair share of the load. In one sense, the excessive demands that have been placed on them to perform have doused the desire (motivation) they originally brought with them when they joined the effort. Collaborators should continually review the requirements for membership to ensure that participants know that contributions can be tailored to the abilities and needs of each individual and that unrealistic demands will be placed on no one.

Simply knowing that a joint project will not continue forever affords a certain amount of comfort to participants. Although a hybrid organization, such as a school-university partnership, might continue indefinitely, collaborative work inside the organization needs to have clear beginning and ending points. Otherwise, participants' commitment can wane. One of the task forces in our partnership, for example, has developed a series of curriculum materials for separate and distinct projects. Over a decade ago, when the task force was just beginning its work, members created a set of classroom materials for teachers and students to prepare them for an exhibit of artifacts from the period of Ramses II that had been brought to our campus. Children who used the materials in their classroom then observed the artifacts.

For the next several years, the task force developed additional curriculum materials in the sciences for teachers in the partnership to use with their pupils. Then when a permanent art museum was constructed on campus, the task force built on its previous work with the Ramses exhibit and helped teachers prepare their students for coming exhibits from Italy and China. In each case, the projects had clear points of beginning and completion. Instructional materials needed to be developed and disseminated prior to the time when the art would be exhibited in the museum; when the exhibit left the museum, the project was essentially completed. Although some task force members participated in all the curriculum projects, others were invited to contribute to just one of the packets. When a project was completed, participation of some task force members came to an end. Some of these participants committed to specific projects precisely because they knew that the collaboration would not go on forever. Helping members understand that collaboration is not eternal will help keep the membership tension in balance.

What about projects that last longer than anticipated and cause some participants to lose interest? How do collaborators deal with members who are performing at unacceptable levels—those whose efforts are actually damaging to the change process? Traditional institutions simply ask these employees to leave the organization by terminating them. But in voluntary partnerships—especially those in which members are not remunerated for their work—termination becomes more complex. The key, we believe, is to "keep the exit door lighted and open." Participants whose needs are not being met by the collaborative should not feel that they must remain permanently engaged in the work. They should also not be made to feel that leaving the organization means that they are uncommitted to the relationships or to the goals of the organization that caused them to join in the first place.

Participants in collaborative educational renewal need to feel that they can opt out of a project when they are unable to make the commitment necessary to achieve the group's goals. After years of intense work, one of the first partner schools in our partnership decided to take a break from being a partner school. We visited with a group of teachers just prior to the decision to change from partner school status. One explained that she was planning not to mentor another student teacher the following year, "I just don't have the energy right now—I just need to have one year when I worry about the children in my classroom and about nobody else." She was opting out and needed to know that she would be respected for her decision, rather than made to feel guilty. She needed to be able to see the exit and know that the door was open.

But she also needed to know that when the time was right, her participation—if she chose to reenter—would be welcomed. She needed to understand that leaving collaborative work can be a temporary situation. After several years of limited involvement in partnership work, she decided to pursue an advanced degree and was invited to take a clinical faculty associate position at the university. As a clinical faculty associate, she would be able to engage in graduate study while simultaneously assisting other teachers in their roles as mentors for student teachers in partner schools. Her own earlier experience as a mentor and as a developer of mentoring programs would benefit other teachers as she helped them learn how to balance their professional roles, as she had done.

Keeping the Balance

If collaborative renewal is successful, pressure will rise to expand the organization. As these pressures increase, collaborators must determine which participants should be invited in and which should be shown the exit door. Membership thus becomes the most potent determinant of success, the one that undergirds all other keys to renewal. When the right participants are engaged in collaborative work, the desired change can be realized—without the right participants, little of worth can be achieved.

Shortly after we created our first partner school, other schools began inquiring about how they might become partner schools. In these early stages of partnership development, our criteria for participation were vague, and this vagueness caused problems for the schools, as well as for the university. The pressure that developed to become a partner school was, as we reflect on it, a positive factor for collaborative renewal. Had no other school pressed for inclusion, the partnership would likely have dwindled and collapsed. But even though the requests from schools were a healthy sign, we still needed to deal with the dilemma of which schools to designate as partner schools and how to determine which schools should retain the designation as time went on.

What we have discovered is that no matter how long a partnership endures, the membership tension must be addressed continually. A partner school that is not engaging in all the agreed-on goals should change its status. If the collaborative work is progressing as it should, the school itself should begin to address each of the goals or temporarily opt out. Regardless of the level of maturity a partnership has reached, performance and motivation never lose their centrality to the work. During times of expansion or consolidation, the organization needs to review these two poles, asking whether each participant—both individual and institutional—is motivated appropriately and performing effectively. This type of constant review will help ensure that the membership tension is kept in balance.

Key #2

Interdependence

On a flight from Long Island to Washington, DC, in below-zero temperatures, the cabin's heating system failed and the pressure in the cabin seemed to be changing. Then, without warning, the compartments opened above our heads and the oxygen masks dropped down in front of our faces. We then heard the flight attendant's voice saying, "The captain assures me that the oxygen masks are not needed. The cabin has not lost its pressurization. Please do not be alarmed." Then a few seconds later—this time with less poise than before—the flight attendant instructed, "I am now told that you should remain calm and place the mask over your mouth and nose and breathe normally. For those with small children, place your own mask on first, and then assist your child."

The flight attendant was telling us in effect that we should take care of our own needs and then care for our children. A parent's first impulse is to help the child first—to meet the other's need before meeting his or her own. But experience has shown that both the parent and child may suffer if the parent faints while attempting to help the child first—then neither may receive the air essential for life.

The dilemma faced by a parent on a troubled flight is similar to the struggles each of us encounters in any type of collaborative work: Whose needs are more important, my own or my colleague's? How do I know when to attend to someone else and when to worry about my own well-being? These are questions of commitment, and we all face them daily. To whom and to what should we commit our time and energy?

The second key to collaborative educational renewal is *interdependence*—the balance point between altruism and self-interest. Symbiotic relationships are all interdependent: Partners meet each other's needs while meeting their own, trading complementary goods that each brings to the table. Covey (1989) describes interdependence as the crowning result of effective living:

> If I am physically interdependent, I am self-reliant and capable, but I also realize that you and I working together can accomplish far more than, even at my best, I could accomplish alone. If I am emotionally interdependent, I derive a great sense of worth within myself, but I also recognize the need for love, for giving, and for receiving love from others. If I am intellectually interdependent, I realize that I need the best thinking of other people to join with my own. (p. 51)

If collaborative work is characterized by relationships of mutuality, participants will develop a high degree of interdependence. They will at times focus on their own needs and at other times concentrate on the needs of their partners. And at all times they will remember the common interests that drew them together in the first place: the need to improve learning and teaching for their students.

Take Time for Lunch

Just as the parent on the troubled flight needs to have oxygen to help the child get oxygen, we must all pay some attention to our own needs if we plan to be of help to anyone else. Self-interest is not equal to selfishness. When being oriented to a challenging leadership position, the first author asked the experienced trainer if he had any final wisdom to share before parting. With a grin on his face, he said, "I will give you the same advice that was given to me years ago when

I was asked to serve in this same position: 'Take time for lunch and the bathroom.' " He was reminding me that I would be of little use to the ones I was supposed to be serving if I had not taken care of my own basic needs.

Once we invited a professor from the University of Paris to visit one of our partner schools. We happened to arrive at lunch hour, so the teachers who greeted us invited us to eat lunch with them. We sat with several other teachers in the faculty lunch room and discussed the activities of the school. After about 15 minutes, teachers began to excuse themselves. The French visitor queried, "Where are you going?" To which one teacher responded, "We need to get back to our classrooms because the children will be returning from recess in about 5 minutes." With an incredulous look on her face, the French professor intoned, "How can you teach children after taking such a short time for lunch? *C'est un horreur.*"

The French, of course, take at least 90 minutes—even in their schools—for the noon-hour break. They see the middle of the day as a time to replenish oneself—not just physically, but emotionally as well. The food in a French lunch is important, but the conversation is the central purpose of the meal. The professor leaned over to me after all the teachers left and said, "I cannot believe that these teachers can face their students again and feel rejuvenated after only a 20-minute break." She was saying in essence that they had not actually taken time for lunch.

Taking time for lunch is simply a figurative way of emphasizing the necessity of caring for one's own needs—needs that extend far beyond physical nourishment. We have seen, for example, university faculty and school educators who gave so much time to collaborative work that they became ineffective and eventually unable to contribute to the common interest. They felt so overwhelmed by the demands of a project or the requests of other partners that they had no time left to meet their own needs—everyone else seemed to have an oxygen mask in place. And the demands on their time were often enticing. The responsibilities did not appear to be burdensome at the beginning of the collaboration, but in fact seemed quite liberating, affording them a welcome change in their professional life. But as the work progressed, they could not find relief from either their usual duties or the new ones they had accepted as participants in a collaborative venture, and the combination became too much for them.

When collaborative renewal is functioning as it should, partners should not require extended breaks. Relationships that are truly interdependent and symbiotic are self-renewing and mutually nourishing. But when one's efforts in renewal are separate from "regular work," overload is inevitable. Collaborative renewal cannot, therefore, be viewed as a segmented part of professional duties; it must be a pervasive presence in one's life. When it becomes a way of thinking and being, collaborative renewal lifts and strengthens participants rather than pulling them down. It helps everyone feel that commitments are complementary rather than divisive.

Serve Together With Idealism

Robert Coles (1993), in *The Call of Service*, discusses "young idealism" and "older idealism" as necessary ingredients when people serve one another. Young idealism, according to Coles, is the kind that leads us to believe that we can change the world, and we need not worry about how our own needs will be met. Older idealism is just as selfless and altruistic, but it is tempered with experience, the knowledge that one's own gifts and time are limited, and a realization that personal motives are at the core of everything we do—particularly acts aimed at helping another human being. Recounting conversations he had with Anna Freud, Coles says,

> For herself, as Miss Freud made clear many times by example, as well as in her writings, idealism or altruism had to do with putting oneself in the shoes of others, absorbing their needs, their vulnerability, their weakness, and their suffering, and then setting to work. We all contend with what psychoanalytic theorists refer to as our libidinal, aggressive, and narcissistic drives and requirements; and in varying degrees most of us contend with a conscience that sets limits on what ought (and ought not) to be done to satisfy our passions, live to the demands of our consciences, and survive—and perhaps prosper—in the world. (p. 205)

In collaborative renewal, participants contribute to each other's lives by "setting to work," as Miss Freud expressed it, on a commonly agreed-on goal. The ultimate recipients of these efforts are the students in the collaborators' schools and universities, but anyone who has engaged in such work recognizes that the greater rewards often come to the collaborators themselves because their offering to others somehow seems to swallow up their own "weaknesses" and "vulnerabilities." Coles goes on to describe an older woman, Alice-Mae, who "spent her life taking care of people" and, when asked why she did it, responded, "I do myself a lot of good by doing good" (Coles, 1993, p. 221).

Although Coles (1993) is not attempting to describe the type of collaborative work one experiences in educational renewal, he captures the concepts critical to one of the balance poles of commitment: altruism, or as he calls it, "idealism." Without a healthy dose of idealism—the desire to help others with no expectation of recompense—collaborative renewal will not succeed. If a partnership is based solely on paid consultancies, shared contracts, and cooperative grants, the renewal process will end when the funding dries up. But if everyone in the collaborative agrees at the outset that their common agenda for change will drive their work, that individual needs of children and youth will determine joint goals, then positive change is possible.

Altruism must constantly be balanced with self-interest, however, or those who are contributing will run out of energy and lose their commitment. When partners find balance between meeting their own needs and the needs of their colleagues, the tensions associated with commitment will bring vitality to the work. Participants will have the needed energy to give and will experience personal growth in the process. Appropriately placed commitment enlivens any organization. There is a certain magic that occurs when people begin to nurture one another spontaneously—for example, a mentor teacher who helps a student teacher who is struggling with a difficult child, or a professor who offers to fill in while a 5th-grade teacher develops a Web-based approach to teaching a history lesson.

When the commitment tension is in balance and interdependence prevails, collaborators become absorbed in each other's needs and fill them almost without thinking. When a computer-assisted approach to early literacy education was being implemented in a partner school, more computers were needed than the principal could provide. When the school lunch directors learned of the need, they offered their computers for use in the project, even though doing so meant that they would need to keep records manually for several months. In another setting, a faculty member in the sciences set aside time for high school students to visit his laboratory and learn how to conduct experiments with an electron microscope—a task that was not in his job description, but one to which he was committed nonetheless.

Stay Focused on the Students

While trying to find a time when a group of university faculty and school teachers could meet to discuss a science education project, one faculty member said that he could not attend because he was teaching during the time that was compatible for everyone else. Another faculty member quickly responded, "Why don't you bring your class to our meeting? After all, it's their education we're trying to improve. We could probably learn something if we listen to what they think about our ideas." The faculty member with the conflict agreed to invite his class, and they all attended the meeting the following week.

We began by asking the students, who were preparing to be secondary science teachers, to describe to us their experience in the program to that point. They eagerly gave us their opinions, discussing the value of some courses and the futility of others. Then we described how we were planning to have them spend time the following summer with the mentor teachers with whom they would be working the subsequent fall term. One teacher immediately began crying, as she described to us her feeling of being overwhelmed with all the requirements that had already been placed on her. "I just don't think I can take on one more thing," she implored.

Other students, though less emotional about the issue, agreed with her comment. They were telling us that they appreciated our good will in trying to improve the program, but we were actually making their life worse instead of better. As a group, we were struck with how strongly the students felt about the issue and how blind we had been to their concern before inviting them to join us. In our well-intentioned effort to strengthen a program, we had lost sight of the individuals we were trying to serve.

Collaborative renewal always aims at improving student learning. The students might be kindergarten children or seniors in a teacher education program, but it is their learning that should always be at the core of collaborative work. Participants need to remind themselves often that student learning gave rise to their collaboration, and that they must continually question any new proposal in light of that one central goal. This common interest is the force behind the key of interdependence.

When participants keep their energies and resources focused on their students, serve together with idealism, and "take time for lunch," the balance between altruism and self-interest will be achieved and interdependence will become a natural part of all collaborative work. In this way, partnerships can sustain themselves because members will "feed each other" while remembering to feed themselves. Throughout the journey, partners continually need to address the tensions associated with the roles each member in the new organization will play.

Key #3

Role Flexibility

When people form new organizations, there is a natural tendency for participants to adopt a group perspective. Teamwork demands that individuals lose some of their individuality. If one team member wants to be the superstar, take credit for group accomplishments, and single-handedly direct the group, other team members soon lose interest in the project. On the other extreme, if participants relinquish their individual identity and decline to use their unique talents and gifts, their contributions to collaborative renewal will be diminished and the group will suffer. Thus, the role flexibility that is necessary in collaborative educational renewal requires participants to balance group perspective with individual identity. If roles become inflexible—because either group perspective or individual identity takes over—the collaborative endeavor is weakened.

The following conversation took place between a university professor of education and a public school administrator who had spent the previous year at the university working full-time for the partnership (T. Howard, personal communication, February 6, 1995):

Professor: Now that you've been with us for a year, I'm interested to know if you've learned anything that will be useful when you return to the district next fall.

Administrator: Are you kidding? I feel like I've learned more this past year than ever—especially about what it means to be a faculty member at this university.

P: What do you mean?

A: I used to think that I understood what faculty at a university did. After all, I've completed two advanced degrees. But I discovered this past year that I didn't have a clue about university life—at least from the viewpoint of a faculty member.

P: Now I'm really interested. So what have you discovered?

A: For one thing, you're busier than I thought. I used to have the idea that university faculty members taught a class or two and then had all this extra time to themselves. As a mentor teacher, I saw faculty members breeze into my classroom and then leave. And I always thought they were leaving quickly so that they could work on their own projects—things that the university appreciated but didn't really demand of them. I envied them in some ways because my time as a teacher seemed to be totally defined. I couldn't even go to the rest room without children following me and knocking on the door while I was inside.

P: What you're saying is music to the ears of professors. We're always complaining that we don't have enough time to do all that is asked of us. So you agree with our "poor-me" attitude!

A: Not exactly. Your time is not as restrictive as ours, but now I'm not sure which is worse—having "time to yourself" when you've got to do an infinite number of things that take more time than you have, or having almost no time to yourself—like teachers in the schools—but not being asked to deliver on it.

The administrator had learned that the role of a university faculty member is different than she had expected. She could not have learned this without attending departmental faculty meetings, assisting with university teaching, and becoming a member of the university community. Her reaction was similar to that of many educators who spend significant time on campus—not as students in university classrooms, but as adjunct or cooperating faculty on loan from the schools. As they assume these new responsibilities, they come to see the role of faculty member as much more complex than they had imagined as students or even as mentor teachers.

Similar surprises come to most university faculty who spend significant time in schools working side by side with teachers or principals. They invariably gain new insights into the professional demands placed on school educators. They come to see the teacher or principal role as a much richer, more complicated position than they had supposed. Helen Stewart (1997) explains the process as follows: "The active moving into and out of various relationships at different times with various combinations of school and university colleagues appears to be liberating in that we continue to refocus and alter our roles and functions" (p. 39).

Stewart (1997) is describing a kind of learning that involves more than caring, more than empathy. She is identifying the unique effects of collaborative educational renewal. When the administrator who had learned to understand the university role returned to the district, not only did she become a champion for the idea of partnership, she also stood up for the needs of university professors in ways that would have been impossible prior to her stay on campus. We often see this kind of reciprocal support coming from those who have spent significant time on the "other's turf."

Following an out-of-state meeting where the first author had participated in formulating plans for partnership evaluation, a school superintendent who arrived late to the session took me aside and said, "Because I was late, I didn't catch where you were from. After listening to your comments, I assume that you must work in the schools because you always seem to speak from their point of view." I was an administrator representing the university, and my taking the schools' "point of view" had been completely subconscious. I believe that the years I have worked in our partnership have helped me to see more clearly through others' eyes.

Walk in Each Other's Shoes

Two faculty members in our university's department of mathematics called the first author one day and asked if I would be interested in observing the work they were doing in a local elementary school. "Would you be willing to bring one of our colleagues with you so that he can also see what we're doing in the school?" asked one. I accepted the invitation and called the other faculty member to coordinate schedules. On the way to the school, the faculty member who was new to partnership work seemed somewhat plaintive as he reflected on his own career, "You know, this is the first time I've ever gone into a school to look at how they teach mathematics. My expertise is actually in quadratic equations—pretty theoretical stuff. No one's even sure if it will ever have any practical value at all."

After we entered the school, the principal escorted us to the classroom where one of my companion's two colleagues was teaching. He was demonstrating the principle of Fibonacci numbers by having the fourth graders count the seed patterns in a large sunflower (see Vajda, 1989). One child exclaimed, "There are 76 seeds in this row, and that's the sum of 29 and 47!" The teacher queried, "Then how many seeds do you predict will be in the next row?" And another child (after adding 76 and 47 on a piece of scratch paper) volunteered, "There should be 123 seeds!" The teacher confirmed the child's response, and we walked to the next classroom, where the other mathematician was teaching a group of fifth graders.

On the way back to the university, my mathematician friend expressed his pleasure at being inside a school watching children study the discipline to which he was devoting his professional life. "I need to spend more time in the schools," he intoned. "All my time with mathematics is spent in my office alone thinking about questions that are pretty remote. Watching these children today reminded me of why I went into the field in the first place." His two colleagues had begun working in the schools for reasons similar to his. They too were mathematicians rather than math educators, but they wanted to become engaged in work that would help the next generation of students develop an affinity for the discipline of mathematics. Nearly all their teaching had been with college-age students, but they were eager to try their ideas with children and teachers in the schools. Their work has shown that the more different two partners are, the more each has to gain by "walking in the other's shoes."

Collaborative educational renewal affords participants the opportunity to try on each other's roles—to see the world from the other's point of view. Whether a mathematician is working with pupils in the fourth grade or a school administrator is functioning as a cooperating faculty member in a university, the opportunity to share some of the responsibilities of an unlike partner offers unique possibilities for individual growth. In neither case, however, does the partner assume all the other person's responsibilities. The school administrator continued to be a school administrator even during her time at the university, and the mathematicians were always viewed as university professors even when they were demonstrating pedagogical approaches in the classroom.

Change Yourself, Not Your Partner

In Goodlad's (1997) book, *In Praise of Education*, he explains the importance of unlike partners retaining their own unique identity:

> Education and religion have been handmaidens in the drama. Often they have been at odds, most frequently when the differences between the two are not recognized, when they have been called upon to play similar rather than different roles. They serve the common good best when they are joined symbiotically, *each in its own rather than the other's idiom.* (Goodlad, 1997, pp. 2-3, italics added)

Whether the partners are religion and education or schools and universities, collaborators must retain their own identity rather than attempting to make professors into classroom teachers or principals into deans. At the moment a schoolteacher complains about a faculty member's inability to take over a 5th-grade classroom, or a university educator derides a 5th-grade teacher for not being familiar with some of the current literature on teacher education, collaborative renewal is in jeopardy. If partners try to make each other over in their own image, the tensions associated with roles will be exacerbated, and commitment to common interests will diminish.

Rather than expecting another to adopt one's own patterns of thinking and behaving, partners should focus on how they themselves can change. The mathematicians value their involvement in elementary schools precisely because the teachers and pupils cause them to reconsider their own pedagogical practice. The mathematicians seek to change themselves rather than their partners. And because the teachers and pupils are also seeking self-improvement, all participants influence one another for the good. Assuming the partner's role—even briefly—is sometimes uncomfortable and always challenging. But because all are committed to the common goal of improving the pupils' understanding of mathematics, they support each other as roles are exchanged. By not trying to change their partners, the mathematicians and teachers allow flexibility in the tasks each one accomplishes and thereby create a balance among the tensions surrounding roles.

Never Forget What You Can Do

One often hears the injunction to celebrate differences. The word *celebrate* means to honor, to give respect to, or to observe. When we celebrate some person or event often and with enough pomp—such as Martin Luther King or Independence Day—the person or event becomes "famous." When Naomi Shihab Nye, a poet with Palestinian and American heritage, visits elementary schools, children often ask her if she is famous. Their question prompted her to write the following poem.

FAMOUS

> *The river is famous to the fish.*
> *The loud voice is famous to silence,*
> *which knew it would inherit the earth*
> *before anybody said so.*
> *The cat sleeping on the fence is famous to the birds*
> *watching him from the birdhouse.*
> *The tear is famous, briefly, to the cheek.*
> *The idea you carry close to your bosom*
> *is famous to your bosom.*
> *The boot is famous to the earth,*
> *more famous than the dress shoe,*
> *which is famous only to floors.*
> *The bent photograph is famous to the one who carries it*
> *and not at all famous to the one who is pictured.*
> *I want to be famous to shuffling men*
> *who smile while crossing streets,*

sticky children in grocery lines,
famous as the one who smiled back.
I want to be famous in the way a pulley is famous,
or a buttonhole, not because it did anything spectacular,
but because it never forgot what it could do.
                                        (Moyers, 1995, p. 328)

In collaborative educational renewal, participants often "forget what they can do"—the contributions they can make in ways that will move the group closer to its goal and edify everyone in the process. Rather than being swallowed up by the group's pressures or standing defiantly on the sidelines saying, "I knew you could not accomplish this without me," organizations that foster flexible roles among their members eventually achieve the common goals that brought them together. Each participant acquires the kind of fame that Naomi Shihab Nye describes in her poem: One becomes famous for suggesting new ideas, another for obtaining administrative approval for a proposed change, and another for implementing the proposal. No one feels unneeded, ineffective, or incapable when all participants remember what they can do.

In a meeting where a group of teachers was discussing the possibility of submitting a journal article, one teacher apologized for her perceived weakness in writing: "Writing is just something I can't do. The rest of you are all good at it, but I'm not." As she finished, another teacher disagreed, "Oh, you're as good as any of us. Why don't you write your version of our experience at the conference we just attended, and let us see it next time." The hesitant teacher accepted the challenge, and during our next meeting, she read to the group her 2-page description of how attending a professional conference had changed her—both personally and professionally. After she finished reading to us, we all sat in silence for a moment. Everyone in the group was visibly moved. Then one said, "And I thought you couldn't write!"

When participants are willing to venture into the uncomfortable, to try on new roles and allow the group to support them, renewal thrives. The teacher could have refused to participate in the writing project—she could have rigidly defined her role as teacher, not a writer—and the collaborative effort would have been less effective. But by trying on a new role with the support of others, she contributed something to the project that no one else was prepared to contribute—she remembered what she could do because others convinced her to attempt an uncomfortable task. And the tensions associated with roles came into balance.

Take Turns Holding
on to the Reins

Role flexibility is particularly important when considering how collaborative groups are led. Old ideas of control and domination must give way to newer notions of shared leadership. In their book, *Leading with Soul*, Bolman and Deal (1995) conclude that

> control is an illusion. It's seductive because it gives a feeling of power. Something to hold on to. So it becomes addictive. It's hard to give up even when it's not working. You just can't start a journey until you let go of habits holding you back. (p. 31)

But even when collaborators give up the need to control each other, someone still needs to take charge in a sense—to call meetings, to suggest a route for the journey ahead. But unlike traditional organizations, voluntary partnerships must not fall into the trap of selecting a traditional leader from the group who has the responsibility to make final decisions and give directions to the other group members. If this occurs, members lose their flexibility to try on new roles, and collaborative renewal is frustrated. The answer for those who participate in collaborative renewal is to take turns leading.

We are not referring only to the perfunctory tasks associated with group work—for example, scheduling, attendance, taking notes—but are including the role of nurturer, the one who brings "grace" to the work setting (see DePree, 1992, pp. 86-87). In collaborative educational renewal, different group members assume one or more leadership roles as the work unfolds: They take turns holding on to the reins. Each gives the other the authority to act, to create, to take the group in a new direction.

When a group of us were planning a science education project, we determined that we wanted high school students, student teachers, and mentor teachers to work together on *real* science. We wanted the collaborative teams to gather data on questions that scientists have not yet answered. One group decided to gather data on a proposed wetlands, another group examined trilobite fossils, another compared the environmental effect of plastic versus paper grocery sacks, and the fourth conducted an experiment on air quality inside the high school.

The teams were free to move in any direction they wished, but someone was always there to give appropriate guidance—a scientist who had some experience in the field, but one who still did not know what the data would show until they had been collected and analyzed. The ones providing leadership or acting as "guides" acknowledged that

> the responsibility of the guide is not to give answers, but to raise questions, suggest directions to explore, and to offer support. "Man is reborn, no longer born of the flesh, but reborn of the spirit, of the inspiration from within and the teacher without." (de Purucker, cited by Bolman & Deal, 1995, p. 170)

As the project proceeded and the proposal was written, each team member helped determine the project's goals. Individuals voiced their own beliefs about the value of the proposed tasks and chose the roles that they would play. We balanced group with individual perspectives by allowing all members to perform tasks of their own choosing. We took turns holding on to the reins—allowing the energy and commitment of the group to lead us in directions that no one in the beginning of the project could have predicted. This type of leadership, as DePree (1989) suggests, is "more an art, a belief, a condition of the heart, than a set of things to do" (p. 148). The authority in such leadership shifts from one member to another as each finds a role and tries it on.

Conclusion

In this section of the book, we have described three tensions that surround relationships in collaborative work: membership, roles, and commitment. Each of these tensions has two poles that must be addressed continually if balance is to be found and the change process is to succeed. When each of the poles is considered and measures are taken to balance them, relationships of mutuality will be strengthened. There are three keys to finding such balance:

1) qualified membership, 2) role flexibility, and 3) interdependence. When these keys are used, the tensions that normally arise in collaborative work will become positive ingredients rather than frustrating inhibitors of the change process.

In this section of the book, we have described the overarching effect of relationships of mutuality and have shown how each key influences these relationships. But collaborative work must go beyond relationships. For renewal to occur, partners must be able to identify some tangible results of their work, some improvement in practice that is evidence of reaching a common goal. Kenneth Strike (1990) calls such results "the goods of accomplishment."

In the next section of the book, we will focus on the tensions that arise as partners begin to produce change—as they focus increasingly on goods of accomplishment. We have identified five such tensions: 1) planning, 2) approach to change, 3) amount of change, 4) evaluation, and 5) giving and receiving. Whereas the tensions discussed previously are connected with relationships, the five tensions that will be treated in the next section all relate to creativity. As in Part I, we will offer a key that can be used to balance each of the tensions associated with the creative process.

PART TWO

Crossing Thresholds to Creativity

As relationships of mutuality form, the stage is set for the creative exchange of ideas, talents, and effort—the ingredients of collaborative change. In this section of the book, we address the creative process that is inherent in such change. The process differs from that of the individual artist or composer cloistered away in a studio, although each participant can experience a type of creative flow enjoyed by the independent artist. Collaboration brings with it, however, a unique invitation to give of one's talents, a way of offering one's gifts for the betterment of the whole.

Before describing the tensions that arise in such work, we will discuss the type of creativity that collaborators must foster if they expect to experience transformative change. To experience this type of enduring change, participants need to recognize the openings that permit creative work to take place and then find ways to cross the thresholds of these openings and engage in collaborative work. The purpose of this section is to identify these thresholds to creativity and to offer suggestions for crossing over the thresholds as collaborative change unfolds.

Gifts and Creativity

All creative acts might be considered gifts. A poet's poem, a musician's performance, an artist's painting—each is a gift from the creator to a broader audience. Each conveys a uniquely individual idea to others for their enjoyment or edification. The giver of the gift seldom knows how the gift will be received. Will the poem or painting be appreciated? Will the performance be applauded? Particularly when the gift is packaged in a new way or when it takes a new form altogether, the artist takes a certain risk in sharing it: Giving such a gift is giving oneself.

Collaborative change rests on creative spirit. The more creative spirit that emerges in a group, the greater the possibility for important change to occur. Thus, all involved in such a change process might be viewed as the givers of gifts. Their work may not result in artistic products, but they are engaged nonetheless in an endeavor that is clearly creative. Seeing the relationship between creativity, gift giving, and change is essential if collaborators are to succeed. Lewis Hyde (1983) explains the relationship as follows:

> Gift exchange [is] a companion to transformation, a sort of guardian or marker or catalyst. It is also the case that a gift may be the actual agent of change, the bearer of new life. In the simplest examples, gifts carry an identity with them, and to accept the gift amounts to incorporating the new identity. It is as if such a gift passes through the body and leaves us altered. The gift is not merely the witness or guardian to new life, but the creator. (p. 45)

Those who collaborate for change have two choices: They can view their efforts as contractual exchanges of labor, or they can see them as gift giving. When one gives a gift, the object is not (or should not be) to obtain a gift in return. One gives because of the need to contribute, to share what might be helpful to those who receive. In contractual arrangements, on the other hand, the parties sign formal agreements up front to protect themselves from being short-changed. We have observed some school-university partnerships, for example, based on consulting contracts between the local school district and the college or university. The district pays a certain amount for university faculty time, and the university releases the requested faculty members and replaces their university function with part-time or adjunct faculty.

Our own partnership was initially based on a 2-page letter of agreement signed by five school district superintendents and the college of education dean. Years later, a more complete agreement was drafted, this time with the help of attorneys from both the schools and the university. Although the formal agreement provides solutions for potential legal problems, it is seldom used by those in the partnership, partly because it characterizes the collaborative effort in a contractual way: "The schools agree to . . . " and "The university agrees to . . . " The spirit of free offerings is somehow lost if partners begin worrying about the degree to which each participant is living up to the formal agreement.

Although we are not suggesting that school-university partnerships avoid formal agreements, we do believe that the people involved must quickly rise above such agreements, or the collaborative enterprise will fail. Rather than worrying about the fairness of each partner's contributions, all must focus on how they themselves can advance toward change, how they can give their gift. When even one person in the group gives freely, others feel compelled to give as well. This contagious gift giving leads to a collective creativity that is essential to collaborative change—especially when the giving occurs at times of transition. Launching a new initiative of any kind requires this kind of selfless giving.

The NSF Project

When our partnership decided to improve the teaching of science and mathematics, we invited an ethnobotonist, a chemist, and a mathematician to discuss possibilities. We began by reviewing a request for proposals from the National Science Foundation (NSF) that called for three-way collaborative projects involving K-12 teachers, teacher educators, scientists, and mathematicians. As the discussion developed, we determined that we wanted to help students experience the kind of science that scientists engage in—to learn to think like a scientist rather than simply memorizing terms for a grade on a test. We wanted students at the university, as well as children and youth in the schools, not only to *do* science but to do *real* science—exploring questions that have not yet been answered.

For some in the group, the idea was a little too lofty. After all, if the teacher did not know the answer to the experiment the students were conducting, would the teacher be able to teach? But the group persisted with the idea and developed four experiments that would be jointly conducted by prospective science teachers, secondary students, science educators, and scientists.

The flurry of "gift giving" that occurred in these early meetings among school and university faculty who were not yet very well acquainted gave life to the project, provided the energy to draft the proposal, and infused participants with a desire to contribute. Professors who had seldom been involved in K-12 schooling gave of their time and expertise; schools agreed to experiment with modifications in their science curriculum; and administrators offered to support the design of the project. The more each participant became involved and committed to the project, the more each was willing to contribute.

Participants were in one sense giving threshold gifts because their contributions came during a transition point—the inception of the project. If any group had been reluctant to contribute, the initiative would have ended. But there was no reluctance, and thus the good will expanded everyone's freedom to create something that went beyond the usual grant proposal. In his definition of collaboration, Schrage (1990) emphasizes the role of creativity: "Collaboration is the process of *shared creation*: two or more individuals with complementary skills interacting to create a shared understanding that none had previously possessed or could have come to on their own" (cited in Fullan, 1993, p. 94).

Those involved in the NSF initiative experienced new understanding because each participant learned from the others. The project made it possible for those involved to transcend self-interest—to give their unique insights for the good of the whole rather than focusing on what they were going to get from the project. As Hugh Nibley (1989) so aptly reminds us, "Our gifts and talents are to be put at the disposal of the human race, not used to put the race at our disposal" (p. 52).

Threshold Gifts

The key in collaborative work is to identify the thresholds that lead to the kind of creativity that will improve teaching and learning.

Seeing the threshold and then crossing it by giving appropriate gifts of oneself will always lead to collaborative change. There are a variety of thresholds in collaborative work, some of which correspond to the thresholds in life—times of important transition.

After sustaining a serious back injury in the bloody battle of Okinawa, the first author's father returned home and began looking for work. His first job offer came from a family friend who owned an automobile business. Hired at the same time was "Skip" Tobata, a young Japanese American who had just been released from an internment camp after spending his late teenage years confined by his fellow Americans. Skip had suffered years of unjustified confinement at the hands of Americans, while my father was watching his fellow soldiers die after being shot by Japanese infantrymen.

Although the two may have had reason to resent each other, they became lifelong friends. In their later years, both developed Parkinson's disease, and they died within 5 months of each other. At Skip's funeral, my father was given a bouquet of long-stemmed roses and asked to place them on his friend's coffin at the appointed time in the services. Noticing that my father had Parkinson's disease, the minister asked if he would need help walking from the bench to the coffin. With quiet resolution, my father responded, "Thanks, but I want to do this by myself."

When the time came, my father stood, shuffled forward, and placed the flowers on the white lace cloth covering the coffin. No words were spoken, just a simple gesture: a final gift to one with whom personal differences had been subsumed in a friendship that even death could not end. Lewis Hyde (1983) calls acts like my father's "threshold gifts," gifts that attend a time of "passage or moment of great change." As Hyde explains:

> [Threshold gifts] are with us at every station of life, from the shower for the coming baby to the birthday parties of youth, from graduation gifts to marriage gifts, from the food offered newcomers and the sick to the flowers placed upon the coffin. Threshold gifts mark the time of, *or act as the actual agents of* individual transformation. (p. 41, italics added)

Hyde's (1983) description of threshold gifts has important implications for collaborative change. By asserting that such gifts not only mark a particular time in one's life but can actually lead to individual transformation, Hyde suggests that gift giving is an integral part of collaborative change. The point is that by understanding the process involved in such gift giving, one can better understand the way the change occurs.

When one of the schools in our partnership agreed to become the pilot site for a new cohort program to prepare elementary teachers, both school and university faculty began giving gifts to one another—sometimes gifts that they had not planned on giving when the program was initially discussed. The primary difference between the new program and the one that it replaced was the time that students spent in the partner school. Rather than receiving the bulk of their instruction in university classrooms, prospective elementary teachers would complete the majority of their course work in the partner school itself, where they could practice new pedagogies immediately with children in the school.

Evaluative data were collected during the first year of implementation. Some of the data caused administrators in both the university and the school to question whether the program should be continued. During a meeting attended by school and university faculty as well as by the school principal and the college dean, the results of the evaluation were presented and all participants were invited to express their feelings about how the program should proceed in the future. At one point, the dean said, "Given the burden that this school-based program seems to place on everyone, I am wondering if we should simply discontinue it and return to the campus-based program."

With no hesitation, one of the school faculty protested,

> I don't think the program should be eliminated. With all its problems, I think we all agree that it's better than the old one. Graduates of this program seem like teachers who have completed their first year of teaching rather than those who have just received their certificate. Sure it's harder for us—and I think it's harder for the faculty from the university too, but it's a stronger program, and we should definitely keep working to improve it.

The dean then asked how many in the group of 35 felt the same as this teacher. All agreed that the program should continue.

In some ways, the change process had put a strain on gift giving. Even though many of the people in the room had been involved directly in the program's design, they struggled as the program was implemented because the nature of the program demanded that they change the way they had been spending their time and required that they communicate more effectively and more frequently with each other as school and university faculty. The partner school had redefined its space, dedicating an entire classroom for the sole use of the student cohort. School faculty were asked by university faculty to change their lesson plans from time to time to accommodate the practice teaching needed by members of the cohort. And university faculty were called on more frequently to demonstrate pedagogical techniques with children in the classroom. Everyone was being asked to "give new gifts."

Because these gifts were being given at the inception of a new program, we consider them similar in nature to the threshold gifts that we each give and receive at important moments in our life. When the teacher disagreed with the dean's offer to discontinue the new program, she was in one sense giving a gift—and simultaneously offering to give more. Faculty from both the school and the university described how the program had improved their teaching. Not only did they see the new program as more effective for the prospective teachers, they saw benefits coming to themselves. Hyde would likely say that because the collaborative change effort was not forced on anyone but was engaged in by individual choice, each participant became both a giver and a receiver of gifts, and by so doing all experienced individual transformation.

How different the meeting with the participants might have been if they had become involved in the new program either by coercion or by promise of financial remuneration. A teacher might have said, "I'll agree to continue working in the program if you in the university will start paying me for all this extra work I'm doing." Had this been the case, the likelihood of transformative change would have been all but eliminated. Hyde (1983) recalls a joke about how market exchange, rather than gift giving, can ensure that threshold gifts will not have their transformative power:

[The comedian] would take a watch from his pocket, check the time, and then say, "It's an old family heirloom. [Pause] My grandfather sold it to me on his deathbed." The joke works because market exchange will always seem inappropriate on the threshold. A man who would buy and sell at a moment of change is one who cannot or will not give up, and if the passage is inevitable, he will be torn apart. He will become one of the done-for dead who truly die. Threshold gifts protect us from such death. (p. 44)

Because virtually every collaborative change initiative occurs at a time of transition from an old way of doing things to a new way, threshold gifts are particularly important. If people forget to give or consciously stop giving during these times of change, the initiative has little chance to succeed.

Teaching as a Transformative Gift

The most common type of gift giving in partnership work is idea sharing. As in the NSF project, participants join together to solve difficult problems by "rummaging around in various places in [one's] mind, and looking at what's there—like rummaging for socks in a drawer" (Moyers, 1995, p. 363). As participants in a collaborative project share their rummagings, they are in fact teaching each other. It is in this type of teaching that creativity thrives and change unfolds.

This is why Hyde (1983) writes of teaching as a transformative gift. The teacher creates instruction, gives it away, and then it has a transforming effect on the learner and, we might add, on the teacher. The one who receives the instructional gift feels a sense of gratitude toward the teacher, and then feels compelled to give the gift away to someone else—to help someone else experience a similar transformation. As Hyde explains:

If the teaching begins to "take," the recipient feels gratitude. I would like to speak of gratitude as a labor undertaken by the soul to effect the transformation after a gift has been received. Between the time a gift comes to us and the time we pass it along, we [experience] gratitude. Moreover, with gifts that are agents of change, it is only when the gift has worked in us, only when we have come up to its level, as it were, that we can give it away again. Passing the gift along is the act of gratitude that finished the labor. The transformation is not accomplished until we have the power to give the gift on our own terms. (p. 47)

In collaborative change, we are constantly teaching each other. A university professor learns from an elementary teacher about the needs of multicultural pupils. Then that same teacher learns from that university professor new strategies for assessing the performance of these pupils. This is what distinguishes collaborative change from individual or private change. When collaboration is working, participants teach one another in transformative ways. They see old things with new eyes because they begin to acquire the other's perspective. A high school English teacher once said,

> I thought I understood the university and what it was all about. But after working inside the place this past year I realized that my understanding was very limited—I saw the university only as a student sees it because that was my experience. Now I see the faculty role differently than I did before. I don't just see the authority or the knowledge faculty possess, but I see the challenges they face in meeting all the expectations that are placed on them (T. Howard, personal communication, February 7, 1995).

The transformation that can come from seeing things from another's point of view is at the heart of collaborative change. When one might question, "Is it really necessary that we meet together to accomplish this task?" another might respond, "Only if you want to change." Teaching as a transformative gift became clear in an opening meeting of our school of education. Included in the meeting were the primary collaborators from the public schools. The presenter, a recognized musician who spends part of each day teaching others to sing, first performed two numbers (offering her gift of singing to the group), taught us about the relationship between music and learning, and then asked, "Is there anyone here who has been experiencing serious health problems who would like some support from the group?"

A woman raised her hand. Many in the group were acquainted with her health problems. Then, without asking the person to describe her problems, the leader simply invited her to take a seat in the center of the room. After the woman had taken her seat, the leader asked that all present stand in a circle around the woman to offer her a gift of music in any way they saw fit—by humming, singing a particular song, or creating a song spontaneously that they thought would be helpful to the one in pain. We all began to sing our own song, some very quietly; as the moments rippled by, the sound became more unified, more harmonious. Everyone began to listen to each other trying to create the most soothing sound possible.

The group singing was transformative for the givers of the gift, as well as for the one to whom the gift was directed. Level of talent was not important. Those who could not hear pitch and harmonize with others simply found another way, perhaps visual, to convey their concern and support for the one seated on the chair. The experience was transforming because it was giving gifts to one in need—briefly seeing the world from her eyes rather than from our own. The session leader had taught us all in a transformative way. Hyde (1983) suggests that the type of community we experienced can occur whenever these types of gifts are offered:

> As an expression of social emotion, gifts make one body of many—almost literally in this case—and when a person comes before us who is in need and to whom we feel an unquestioning emotional connection, we respond as reflexively as we would were our own body in need. (p. 66)

Creativity and Change

Although the group leader could have asked us all to sing a familiar song in unison, she requested that we create our own melody or gesture—one that would communicate our desired message to the person we encircled. She was asking in one sense that we engage in collaborative change, which always demands a measure of creativity. The creativity itself cannot be viewed as the desired change. It is the energy behind the change, the light that guides it. In the NSF example, the creative sharing led to a proposal for change. But once the application was approved, participants needed to enact their creations—live them out—before the process was complete.

Educators often want to short-change the creative phase, moving directly to implementation. But good ideas need to be nourished, and nourishment—especially by a group—requires time. The creative energy that characterized the NSF project in its early stages continued to effect change as the project developed. Because the change was transformative, teaching practice has continued to evolve long after funding for the initiative has ended. For example, secondary students from schools that were not involved in the original project are now participating in the study and creation of wetlands in their communities—all as a result of educators accepting the invitation to help students experience science the way scientists themselves experience it.

Creativity and
Collaborative Renewal

We heard a prominent educator say recently that the collaborative movement in education will diminish and eventually die because "it just takes too much effort for everyone." He was basing his perception on the old accounting principle that when cost exceeds benefits, participation will flag and could stop altogether (M. R. Swain, personal communication, February 6, 1998). We agree that if a partnership is built on the market model—where each participant's contribution is measured against others' contributions in dollars or time—the collaborative will likely wither away. That is why we emphasize the centrality of gift giving, creativity, and thresholds in collaborative renewal. Partners who identify thresholds and then contribute their ideas and talents to create something better will, we believe, endure.

In fact, without this type of collaborative renewal, public education itself will eventually cease to exist. The teachers we need for tomorrow's schools must have increased contact with pupils in the classroom. But they must also forge relationships with parents, university faculty, and school administrators. They must learn how to teach in transformative ways not only in the classroom but in the conference room and the lunch room as well. In short, they must be allowed to give their gifts and talents for the betterment of the whole. If collaborative work diminishes, their opportunities to give also diminish. Our response, therefore, to those who see collaboration as a passing fad is to remember that giving—which is the core ingredient of collaborative work—is a basic human need. People can survive for only a short period of time without it. As poet and novelist May Sarton has said:

> There is only one real deprivation, I decided this morning, and that is not to be able to give one's gift to those one loves most. . . . The gift turned inward, unable to be given, becomes a heavy

burden, even sometimes a kind of poison. It is as though the flow of life were backed up." (quoted in Hyde, 1983, p. 146)

Even when one is allowed or encouraged to cross the threshold and give creative gifts that benefit the whole, questions arise and tensions can ensue. These tensions are part of the creative process, part of attempting something that predecessors have been afraid to try. They can be debilitating only if they are allowed to tip too far in one direction. When they are kept in balance, risk taking flourishes, creativity thrives, and renewal prospers.

Key #4

Nurtured Development

There is a crucial difference between societal movements to re-form education and the kind of renewal we are calling for in this book. Reform movements begin and end, often falling short of the original goals that gave rise to the movement. Renewal, however, is a continous process, a way of being, that has no discrete point of departure or destination. Speaking of the most recent school reform movement, John Goodlad (1997) says:

> The decade from approximately 1985 to about 1995 may prove to be in our history the years of the most precipitous decline in the public association of the school and the American Dream and, indeed, of faith in both. The prospect is replete with ironies, most of them arising from misplaced expectations and myopic concep-tions of cause and effect. That school reform failed is quite obvious. Whether and where the schools may have failed is not nearly as decipherable. (p. 72)

Coming from one who has been in the middle of the reform movement from its inception, Goodlad's (1997) assessment is particularly compelling. If he were a distant observer documenting reform efforts simply for the sake of historical interest, one might question his conclusions, attributing his perceptions to certain biases or misunderstandings to which "outsiders" often hold. But he is no outsider. He has lived the past decade as one of the nation's foremost supporters of educational renewal.

By concluding that the present reform movement has not achieved its aims, Goodlad (1997) is not saying that we should abandon the idea of public schooling and create something totally different in its place. He is, we believe, trying to help his readers see that laying all the burden of education on schools will never work in a democracy. Rather than abandoning the schools, he is actually calling for greater commitment on the part of everyone in the society to contribute to the education of the young. Some of these contributions will be in cooperation with schools; others will be complementary activities emanating from the broader community. But in each case, those who are committed to the next generation of learners will need to strengthen their collaborative ties. They will need to plan together in ways that will lead to improvements in how the young are taught.

One of the keys to this kind of renewal is *nurtured development*. Nurturing implies that colleagues will sustain each other by offering the precise type of support that each participant needs at a given moment. As this type of nurturing expands, the institution (e.g., the school) improves. Rather than seeing the school as an organization that needs some quick fix, or viewing teachers as defective professionals who must be remediated, participants nurture one another. Nowhere is this more evident than in the planning process itself.

Table 1 on p. xx of this volume shows that nurtured development is the balance point between spontaneous renewal and planned change. It acknowledges that both spontaneity and systematic planning are necessary in collaborative change, but implies that when a partnership moves too far to either pole, nurturing will cease and the joint effort will be in jeopardy. Too much spontaneity means that one collaborator—other than the one with the new idea—will be ignored; too much systematic planning means that the goals and strategies take preeminence over individual needs. In each case, nurtured development decreases, and the planning process suffers. If the tensions that develop around planned change and spontaneous renewal are handled effectively, participants will assist one another in the planning process, causing teaching and learning to improve.

To balance the tensions associated with the planning process, we suggest that collaborators a) recognize the thresholds, b) encourage good conversation, and c) decide with discernment. These approaches will lead to nurtured development, releasing participants' creative potential and laying the foundation for the kind of change that will transcend any movement or supersede any mandate.

Recognize the Thresholds

To foster nurtured development in the planning process, participants must learn to recognize the thresholds that will lead to creativity and eventually to change. These thresholds are akin to what Myers and Simpson (1998) have called "points of intrusion—convenient places to initiate experimentation and to test the efficacy of new ideas" (p. 12). The most common meaning of the term *threshold* is "the sill of a doorway" that one crosses to enter a home. But it can also refer to "the lower limit below which a stimulus is not perceptible" (Simpson & Weinere, 1989). A dentist who decides not to numb someone's tooth before drilling might say, for example, that the patient has a "very high pain threshold"—meaning that the drilling must become intense before the patient is bothered by the pain.

When a change feels as if it is being forced, the group's threshold has been ignored, and participants resist—either passively or by openly sabotaging the effort. Rather than allowing collaborators to move with the change at their own pace and in their own way, leaders lose patience and coerce the group into conforming to an edict or a mandate. The clearest examples of forced change are the attempts of government to legislate school reform. When a new law is not in the best interest of children, educators and community members usually find a way to ignore or subvert it.

When thresholds are acknowledged, participants are not only drawn to the change process but feel compelled to contribute. Approximately 1 year after we piloted a new school-based teacher education program, a group of mentor teachers approached the university faculty in their school and said,

We have been impressed with the kind of growth that the university students are experiencing in this new program. But some of us are beginning to ask ourselves: What about us? Can we as teachers experience that same kind of growth? Several of us are eager to seek another degree, but we want to do it in the same way that these students are pursuing their undergraduate degree. We want a school-based master's program—one that would let us ask questions about our own teaching practice.

A meeting was scheduled by the executive director of our partnership that included the interested teachers, the school principal, the dean, and other university faculty. Most of the meeting was spent listening to the teachers express their desire for professional development. No one in the meeting knew what the curriculum would be for the type of school-based master's program the teachers were calling for. But university and school participants agreed that such a program was worth exploring. Collaborators were recognizing a threshold of change, articulating a possibility for improving the professional development of teachers while strengthening the graduate offerings of the university. Like all thresholds, this one opened the way for new participants, such as other faculty, to join in the collaborative work. The meeting ended with an agreement between the teachers and the university to design such a program.

The more collaborators look for these openings to creativity, the more positive the change process becomes. For example, the director of the microscopy laboratory at our university regularly invites high school students into his lab to conduct their own experiments with the electron microscope. As some of these students completed their studies and published their results, he could see the benefits of providing this type of resource to these nonuniversity students. Working with others, he obtained an electron microscope for a junior high partner school, with the goal of exposing as many science students to this powerful research tool as early in their school experience as possible. The placement of the microscope in the school has caused students and faculty alike to see science more as an invitation to think creatively than as a set of terms to be memorized.

Encourage Good Conversation

Parker Palmer (1993) encourages "good talk about good teaching." His point is that we are changed by the conversations we have with others. In today's world of pocket planners and efficiency models, the time devoted to collegial conversation has dwindled, and in the process, our society has been weakened. Collaborative change is impossible without engaging in what we call "good conversation"— conversation that leaves both parties feeling more able, more appreciated. It causes each person involved to reach a little higher, risk a little more. Good conversations begin on the threshold to creativity and continue to refresh collaborators as they work to improve teaching and learning.

Some engage in good conversation regularly and naturally, whereas others may prefer to complain and find fault. All efforts in collaborative change need to make space for good conversation. One way of making this space is to invite at least some participants who will naturally help foster this kind of dialogue. E-mail and online group communication services can enhance communication across school and university boundaries, but there are times when face-to-face contact is essential. Personal meetings must be more than the typical professional meeting where agendas dictate the content of the conversation. Participants need time to talk about their desires for change without feeling as if they are infringing on an agenda that already has more items than can possibly be covered in the allotted time.

Three zoology professors on our university campus have begun to collaborate on a cell biology course that each one teaches. They first came together when one professor wanted to see how another was teaching a certain topic, so he attended the colleague's course. Following the first visit, the two found themselves discussing pedagogical issues, as well as course content, in ways that enriched both. They were engaging in good conversation. Their discussions were so productive that they began attending each other's classes regularly, and they invited a third professor to join in their collaborative venture.

As they continued to discuss their course, they decided that they could actually save preparation time if they joined forces to teach the same section. Part of the agreement was that all three would attend all class sessions, and they would continue to talk to one another about the course and suggest ways they could improve it.

They determined that their main purpose in the course was to prepare students to solve real problems related to the biology of cells, problems akin to those scientists grapple with. So they agreed that they would limit their lecture time and replace it with problem-solving practice in each class period. They are convinced that students are learning more biology and are more able to use their new knowledge to solve real problems. No university leader mandated that they get together. They came together on their own for the sole purpose of improving their teaching, and each professor attests to the benefits he has received from the experience—all because they made time for good conversation.

Use Shared Discernment

Good conversation can lead to effective collaborative planning, but only if participants listen intently and value each person's contribution. We once heard a colleague say, "It was when the institution stopped valuing my ideas that I no longer wanted to be a part of it." This person gradually felt misplaced within the institution—as if he were outside its walls observing the creative process taking place on the inside but unable to participate in it.

Collaborative renewal cannot occur unless each person in the group values the contributions of all other members. This does not imply that everyone must agree all the time—far from it. One way that nurtured development increases is for members to play off one another—to voice an alternative viewpoint, to communicate with honesty and openness, and to give what has been called "sweet counsel" (kind correction) when appropriate. One who feels institutional abandonment, such as our colleague, develops it not because others disagree with him, but because they utterly ignore him.

Nurtured development demands a type of collective decision making because collaborative change is not a solo venture. But we believe that the kind of change that is needed in our institutions of learning—private or public, schools or universities—requires more than the shared decision making or participatory leadership that is often espoused (see Clift et al., 1995). We prefer to call it *shared discernment*. Discernment involves more than arriving at a decision that everyone in the group accepts. A discerning person is one who is constantly engaged in the search, one who knows that the right decision will eventually emerge.

A discerning group does not base its planning on compromise or tactics for wooing reluctant group members to a particular position. Members assume that there is a better way of doing things, and that they will find it together. They also agree that until they all feel that a proposal is right and good, they will not pursue it. Rather than voting on an issue and allowing the majority to rule, the group assumes that it will achieve consensus—that by weighing every option and pondering every suggestion, members will gradually discern what is best. This kind of decision making is integral to the functioning of what has been called "morally based communities of learners" (Myers & Simpson, 1998, p. 17).

At one point in the development of our school-university partnership, administrators in partner schools requested that the university review its principal preparation program and consider revising it. Professors in the department of educational leadership accepted the challenge. But rather than mailing surveys to graduates, analyzing the data, and revising certain courses, they invited school educators to review the program from the bottom up. No part of the program was considered off limits. Anyone could make a comment about any aspect of the methods for preparing school leaders. Even some of the recently admitted students were invited to participate in revising the program they would complete.

Experienced principals, professors, teachers, and graduate students all engaged in a type of planning that balanced the tensions associated with planning. The group realized that it would eventually need to identify courses, assign faculty to those courses, and fit all instructional segments into an effective sequence. But it also wanted to foster spontaneity—to allow participants to suggest anything that came to their minds. The group gradually developed a program that responded to everyone's needs: providing for a more effective student selection procedure, a closer tie between theory and practice, and improved mentoring of prospective principals.

As the planning group developed an improved program, members experienced personal and professional growth in the process. Members did not feel ignored or excluded, regardless of their position. After serving for several years as a principal of an elementary partner school, one graduate of the new program exclaimed, "I couldn't believe that the university was actually asking my opinion about what I hoped for in graduate study. I guess I shouldn't say this, but it really felt good—just for a few moments—to tell the university what to do."

This principal experienced the kind of openness, the kind of listening, that must be present if the tensions of change are to be balanced. She did not expect the group to take every suggestion she

offered—she may not even have wanted to hold to her own suggestions at times—but she knew that the group was listening and that
her participation was influencing the final outcome. The group welcomed different views, discussed each as it entered the conversation,
and then made decisions with discernment, choosing the path that,
in the members' shared vision, would lead to stronger, more effective
principals who would foster improved learning for students.

Key #5

Inquiring
Change Agentry

The act of creation always begins with a question. A scientist posits a new relationship between variables, an artist imagines a new use of color or texture, a poet combines words in a new way. Whether the one creating can articulate it or not, a question is always imbedded in the process of making something new. As the questioning process improves, so does one's ability to create. But the outside appearance of a question does not necessarily correlate with good creative work. One scientist might judge another's hypothesis to be brilliant but not be impressed at all with the research method or the results.

When one sees a creative act gone awry, it is usually seen as a skill deficiency; for example, the teacher does not know how to teach, the principal does not know how to lead, the athlete does not know how to play the game. But there is typically more to it than that. Motives often supersede skill as a determinant of creative activity—the artist who is driven purely by market pressure, the teacher who is grinding out 5 more years because "I can't give up the retirement pay."

So although questions are central to creative work, the degree to which the question matters to the person is of paramount importance.

The kind of collaborative renewal we need in schools and universities demands not only that certain questions be asked but that they be asked in certain ways. Such questions need to come from inside the person rather than imposed by someone else. They need to grow out of the person's experience rather than be contrived to meet an artificial requirement. These can be called "questions of the heart" because they spring from the center of one's being, capturing the individual until an answer has been found (see Osguthorpe, 1996b).

Examples of good questions with pure motives abound in some educational settings. These institutions have learned how to identify thresholds by encouraging members in the organization to ask questions that will lead to genuine creative work and eventually to real change. The questions are part of the gift giving that collaborators exchange. The teachers who were calling for a new type of master's program were asking this kind of question, as were the principals who suggested that the leadership preparation program be revised.

Champions and Critics

In most collaborative renewal efforts, someone assumes the role of the champion. This person is committed to the change process and believes in the approach being taken. Our partnership would not have survived without the contributions of those who championed its purposes. From its inception, however, our partnership has also had its critics—university faculty and school educators who look at the partnership and judge it as either ineffective or destructive. At times the champions and critics face off in open debate, but these discussions are seldom fruitful. Champions often leave more convinced than ever that the partnership is worthwhile, and critics leave more skeptical of its potential.

Both the critic and the champion want to see things improve. Both believe in change. But their approaches to change are at opposite poles, and if either side takes over, collaborative change is in jeopardy. The champion's fervor to contribute can cause others to devote time to a less-than-worthy effort. And the critic's constant badgering can engender enough negativism in a group that not even the most valuable initiative can succeed. Collaborative renewal demands that members play both the champion and the critic role, but if the group swings too far in either direction, the tension in the group will become so debilitating that the possibility of change is seriously limited.

A Balanced
Approach to Change

The midpoint between champion and critic is the *inquiring change agent*, a person who wholeheartedly supports worthy initiatives but who stands back and questions the results. As they feel impressed to do so, members trade roles, at one time arguing that a particular project be pursued, at another time raising questions about its worth. The ability of members to move back and forth between these two roles depends on their inner commitment to the change process and their openness to new information.

To achieve balance in an organization's approach to change, we offer four suggestions: 1) Foster a culture of inquiry, 2) receive questions as gifts, 3) experience edification, and 4) blend the champion and critic roles.

Foster a Culture of Inquiry

Examining school culture has been identified as a key to understanding how to improve the organization by a variety of educational writers (Sarason, 1982, 1996; Taba, 1955). Anyone who has been inside more than one school knows that the atmosphere differs from one school to another. The principal alone casts a definable hue over every aspect of teaching and learning in a school. Some are warm and eagerly welcome visitors into their schools; others seem to wish visitors would stay away. The teachers in one school might evidence a high degree of collegiality, whereas those in another isolate themselves from each other.

If educators want to improve the way they are conducting schooling, they need to establish and sustain a culture of inquiry. Such a school questions everything; no topic related to teaching and learning is off limits. If teachers believe that the curriculum is not effective, the academic schedule is not conducive to learning, or the role in mentoring student teachers is not what it should be, they openly discuss their opinions. But as Sarason (1982) points out, teachers seldom have time to consider new ideas in depth. Their day is full of teaching and preparation activities. This assessment holds true today.

Even with increased emphasis on the study of one's own teaching practice and the encouragement to conduct action research in the classroom, teachers are still unlikely to find the time they need to reflect on and improve their pedagogy and design. That is why the structure of the school day needs to be addressed if schools are to change their culture in any substantive way. Teachers need to be given time to talk to each other, and some of that time needs to occur during the school day. In our partnership, for example, we try to find ways for teachers to discuss issues on an extended basis. Teachers bring their questions to inquiry groups and explore together solutions to their questions. One inquiry group focused a significant amount of time on how to work effectively with children with attention deficit disorder. Another group focused on how to provide full inclusion for students with disabilities in a junior high school.

The kind of culture we are talking about is one in which teachers, students, and parents can all ask questions that matter to them, a culture that invites everyone to become an inquiring change agent. We are convinced that, although this may be difficult to assess directly, it is one of the most important factors in collaborative renewal. Such schools are places where educators can say with Maxine Greene (1995), "we look, we wonder, and the questions come and batter us" (p. 143).

Receive Questions as Gifts

A group of early childhood educators in France came together approximately 20 years ago in an informal inquiry group to discuss their own teaching practice (see Osguthorpe & Osguthorpe, 1996). As they questioned the amount of structure and the type of discipline that were the hallmarks of French maternal education, they gradually formed an alternative philosophy of teaching that they wanted to implement. As their beliefs took shape, they determined that the best way to test them would be to create a new school centered around their newly articulated philosophy. Somewhat like those who organize charter schools in the United States (see Nathan, 1996), the group obtained government approval and began accepting children into the school.

As with most substantive change initiatives, the French educators were surprised with the challenges that faced them during the first year of implementation:

> During the first few weeks, we experienced a sort of chaos in the school. Children were confused about where they should be and what they should be doing, and teachers were equally confused. We had agreed on some basic principles, but we hadn't determined exactly how to put those principles into practice. We met every day after school during those first few weeks to hammer out how we were going to handle the problems that were arising. We never let go of the principles that brought us together. We knew that we were on the right track—we just needed to decide how to keep the train moving without getting derailed. (Langevin teachers, personal communication, October 27, 1994)

These French educators were not afraid of questions. In fact, they saw the inquiry process as their only way out of the chaos that their newly implemented change had wrought. They described those early meetings as animated, even heated, discussions during which one teacher might challenge another's suggestion until the group could find common ground. Although each was an independently strong teacher, each valued the others' viewpoints. Rather than seeing questions as personal attacks or as ploys for one individual to gain power over the group, the teachers came to see questions as gifts. By questioning practice as a group, each became more effective with children in their classrooms. And as each became more effective, the school itself was transformed.

If the group had denied even one of its teachers the privilege of questioning the school's direction, the culture of inquiry would have eventually disintegrated and renewal would have ceased. But members kept the culture alive by welcoming each other's questions as gifts, encouraging experimentation, and withholding judgment until an individual teacher opened the way for dialogue. By emphasizing their own brand of inquiring change agentry, members were able to balance the tensions associated with their desire to improve learning for French children.

Visitors to this school could seldom articulate its unique features immediately, but they usually commented on the unusual amount of vigor and spirit in the school. Paraphrasing from Hyde (1983):

> Because a circulation of [questions] has a cohesive or synthetic power, it is almost as a matter of definition that we say such increase is a gift (or is the fruit of the gift). [When questions are received as gifts], they are the agents of that organic cohesion we perceive as liveliness. (p. 150)

Experience Edification

Collaborative renewal cannot end, of course, with questions—questions are simply the underlying energy that keeps the change process alive. Participants must strengthen each other in ways that will provide members of the group with the courage needed to venture into the unknown. If approached in the right way, this type of discourse can be more than intellectually stimulating or personally enlightening: It can also be edifying. For children and teachers alike, the French maternal school was an edifying place to be, a place where everyone was made to feel more able to cope with problems, a place where everyone felt cared for (Osguthorpe, 1997).

Although the term *edify* has largely fallen out of use in today's schools, it captures what most would like education to embody. The first meaning of the word is "to build or construct." The French verb *edifier* is used much like the verb *erect* in English: "to construct a building." But the second meaning of the word focuses more on the function of spiritual strengthening, drawing a person closer to "virtue." Briefly stated, *edify* means "to build up the soul." (Simpson & Weinere, 1989, p. 71).

The balance point of inquiring change agentry implies that participants edify one another. Their questions can have an edifying effect, but their responses to questions must also carry that same edifying message. This does not mean that disagreements are covered up or suppressed. To the contrary, such an exchange can be the most edifying of all if participants are on a mutual hunt for the right answer—if they are open to one another's differences and willing to open themselves to a new way of doing an old thing.

To foster this kind of open dialogue among those involved in the renewal process, John Goodlad instituted an associates program in which collaborators from one partnership joined with those from another to discuss the bedrock issues associated with change. Prior to attending the four week-long meetings, educational leaders from the 15 partnerships then in the National Network for Educational Renewal (NNER) were encouraged to read certain books or articles related to collaborative renewal. Each participant also designed an inquiry project as a result of the meetings—one that would apply directly to current renewal efforts. Following the year of meetings, one superintendent in our partnership remarked that he had never participated in a more stimulating professional development experience, partly because he had acquired new ideas that he could put to work in his own district, but also because he had experienced a sense of self-renewal that would permit him to put his new ideas into practice. In short, he had been edified.

Because of the success of the NNER Associates Program, our partnership decided to implement its own version locally. This is now becoming a permanent part of our consortium. Superintendents, arts and sciences faculty, teacher educators, and university leaders are invited to participate each year in extended discussions that bear directly on partnership work. As a result of our associates program, new initiatives have been implemented, such as a program to help teachers become more effective with students who have limited English proficiency. Such programs become places where transformative gifts can be given, where participants can think new thoughts and edify each other, where they can become inquiring change agents.

Become a Critical Champion

When members of a group modify their perceptions because of their own inquiry or because of someone's response to their inquiry, they have in essence accepted another's gift. And when they receive such a gift, they become compelled to reciprocate. Reciprocity is inherent in renewal. But because participants approach change differently, most need some kind of encouragement in both giving and receiving. The critic may dismiss any idea that comes from a champion. And the champion may never come to appreciate the critic's comments. The fundamental question is whether these two roles can be combined in one individual. Can a person be both supportive and hesitant at the same moment or in the same conversation?

When our partnership was in the process of rethinking the elementary teacher preparation program, we intentionally brought together stakeholders who had known differences of opinion about how the program should be changed. Not surprisingly, those who held the firmest views about how a certain course should be deleted or expanded were usually those who knew the least about the other courses required to complete the major. As these participants learned more about the whole program, they gradually softened their demands for more credit hours in their particular content areas. Once participants were able to agree that art or dance should not be viewed as more important than literacy, or that math should not be considered as more valuable than science, the large group of planners became more willing to consider new ideas.

To become an inquiring change agent, one must come to see things from the other's perspective, even when that perspective seems in total opposition to one's own. During a planning session in which student teacher mentoring was being discussed, a 4th-grade teacher said,

> My real problem is that out of the 20 students in the cohort, I believe about 10 of them are teachers we would want to hire, about six or seven will probably succeed in time, and two or three should be counseled out of the profession. The university is just not doing its job in counseling some people out.

Looking somewhat surprised, a university faculty member responded, "So you're saying that the problem student is totally the responsibility of the university? What is your role as a mentor teacher in helping someone decide to pursue another major?"

The teacher had never considered it her role to counsel a problem student out of the teacher education major, but when the question came, she accepted it. She agreed that she had not played as central a role as she should have in the evaluation of students completing practica in her classroom. She began to see the problem from the other's point of view, and in the process, both the teacher and the teacher educator began trading roles as champion and critic. They were each in turn identifying weaknesses in the way prospective teachers were being educated, but each was also openly supportive of the venture. They were acting as critical champions—participants who could be genuinely supportive of an idea while simultaneously offering suggestions to improve it.

Key #6

Disciplined Openness

Regardless of one's approach to change, collaborators continually feel pressure to put into immediate practice every good idea that emerges and the pressure to perfect what has already been put into place. Thus, some members of the partnership push to expand in every conceivable direction, whereas others want to reduce the size and number of initiatives to obtain greater "focus." We call the balance point between these two poles *disciplined openness*, a mindset that allows participants to consider a new idea while contemplating how the idea fits with current collaborative work.

When an organization attempts to focus all its energy on maintaining current practice, it denies itself the very nourishment it needs to survive. Much as a magnifying glass can burn a hole in a piece of paper when focusing sunlight continually on a single spot, collaborative energy can burn itself out by focusing too much attention on a single initiative. Likewise, the organization can disintegrate if it attempts to do everything for everybody.

If our partnership has leaned too far in one direction, it would likely be our willingness to embrace more ideas than we can possibly execute successfully. Our coordinating council, composed of associate deans from the school of education and associate superintendents from the five partner school districts, has often acted as a clearinghouse for partnership proposals. But the approval process is never easy. And council members often wonder if the proposals they approve are integrated strongly enough into the overall mission of the partnership. The council has often seen similar proposals coming from several sources, each with no awareness of the other's work. This led the organization's leaders to propose a single partnership-wide initiative to improve literacy education both in the schools and in the teacher education program.

At the meeting during which the superintendents and deans agreed to pursue a large-scale project on literacy education, participants considered the needs of their districts, discussed possible options to meet those needs, and then agreed on a basic strategy to follow and a plan for carrying out the strategy. They did not limit partnership work to the literacy initiative, but agreed that if each district, along with the university, contributed to the project, more could be accomplished than if each district sponsored its own separate effort. They were in the process of giving to one another. But they were giving in a disciplined way because they recognized their limitations. They knew that their various organizations did not have infinite amounts of money or time to devote to the effort, but they committed themselves and their organizations to the goals of the project nonetheless.

These participants were using the key of disciplined openness to resolve the tension between too much and too little focus. They knew the history of the partnership, and they knew the history of their own institutions. These bases of knowledge allowed them to plan in a way that would benefit rather than damage students. They knew people in their organizations who could contribute to the initiative, and they devised ways to provide these capable individuals with the time needed to make their contribution. The group drew on relationships of mutuality that had already been formed as they discussed the new collaborative venture.

Although no one in the group articulated the effort in exactly these terms, each member was using the key of disciplined openness by doing the following three things: 1) building on past gifts, 2) viewing time as a friend, and 3) being generative and provident.

Build On Past Gifts

In planning the literacy initiative, leaders recognized that successful collaborative efforts draw on work that has already been accomplished. Rather than seeing tradition as an enemy, those who contribute to collaborative renewal build on past practices as they plan for the future. Although they eschew damaging or unhealthy traditions, they see good traditions as thresholds that lead to productive change.

When our partnership was young, a group of school and university faculty joined together to prepare school-age children and youth for an archaeological exhibit based on the life and times of Ramses II that was coming to the university. To house the exhibit, the institution had to construct a temporary facility because it had no art museum. A curriculum packet was written and distributed throughout the partnership. Special programs were created so that the maximum number of students would be able to study the curriculum materials and then come to campus to view the exhibit.

The Ramses effort was so successful that several years later, when the university completed construction of its new art museum, members of this same group designed similar programs for an Etruscan exhibit and then for an exhibit on the emperors of China. With each successive project, the number of participating students increased. Planners of these curriculum materials were building on past efforts—not in a purely linear way, but in creative ways that led to improvements in the learning that museum visitors experienced.

View Time as a Friend

Collaborative work always seems to be moving either too quickly or too slowly. Those who pull on the "expansion" cord cause many in the organization to feel like they are running to catch up. Those who pull on the "focus" cord frustrate others who want to implement a new idea immediately. These tensions are nearly always present in such work and should not be viewed as enemies. They actually provide some of the energy that is needed in any organization that engages in collaborative renewal.

Shortly after our partnership established its first partner elementary school, other schools became interested in the designation. At the time, we had not developed a systematic way of reviewing such requests, so one by one, schools were invited to become full-fledged partner schools. Reflecting on the experience, most in the partnership feel that we moved too quickly. We were probably pulling on the expansion side a little too enthusiastically.

As time passed, the partnership designed an application form for those wishing to become partner schools. The form itself discouraged some would-be applicants—particularly those who saw such a designation simply as a way to receive more benefits from the university. And some of the schools that had already received the designation decided to become focus schools and emphasize one or two of the goals of a partner school rather than all four, as discussed in Chapter 1, "Key 1: Qualified Membership."

The tension between embracing every new idea and being highly selective must eventually lead collaborators to the midpoint of disciplined openness if the venture is to succeed. By using the term *disciplined*, we are implying that collaborators restrict each other by withholding rewards or inflicting punishment. The type of openness we are suggesting is the type that comes from the creative spirit. Augustin Lesage (1876-1954), a French coal miner who felt that he was called to leave the mines to become a painter, explained the creative process as a journey of spiritual guidance:

> A picture comes into existence detail by detail, and nothing about it enters my mind beforehand. My guides have told me: "Do not try to find out what you are doing." I surrender to their prompting . . . I follow my guides like a child. (quoted in Maizels, 1996, p. 56)

Like other creative people, Lesage was articulating the relationship between the product of his work and the work itself. Sculptors talk of seeing a form when they look at the rough-cut stone or the newly cut piece of timber. Musicians speak of melodies entering their minds at odd moments. Mozart, for example, explained his composing experience as follows:

> When I feel well and in a good humor, or when I am taking a drive or walking after a good meal, or in the night when I cannot sleep, thoughts crowd into my mind as easily as you could wish. Whence and how do they come? I do not know and I have nothing to do with it. Those which please me, I keep in my head

and hum them; at least others have told me that I do so. (quoted in Noddings & Shore, 1984, pp. 72-73)

To both Mozart and Lesage, time was a friend rather than an enemy of their creative process. Their openness to the creative spirit could not have occurred as it did if they had been burdened with the kind of artificial deadlines that our culture tends to impose. Their discipline was an inner discipline rather than a set of sanctions that came from others interested in their work. The type of discipline that it took for Mozart to select the tunes that pleased him or for Lesage to listen to the guides that gave him the details of his paintings is the kind of discipline we are suggesting for partnership work. It is a kind of discipline that allows collaborators to open themselves to new possibilities, to understand the messages that their students are sending them, and to cross over the threshold to creativity.

Be Generative and Provident

When the first author was on the faculty at National Technical Institute for the Deaf (NTID), Ralph Tyler visited the institution to address the faculty and staff as a member of our national advisory committee. His remarks are still fresh in my mind even though he delivered them two decades ago. I recall the beginning of his speech:

> I have been impressed with the enthusiasm, the intellectual energy I have felt as I have interacted with you the past few days during my stay in your institution. There is no question that you are committed to doing good creative work that will make life better for the hearing-impaired students you came here to serve. But let me warn you that keeping this kind of intellectual energy in an institution is difficult. I have served on a number of other national advisory groups, and I have seen this same type of initial creative zeal gradually decline as the majority of faculty become more concerned about salary and retirement benefits than they are about doing good research. I urge you to take measures to ensure that this kind of decline does not happen here.

Although Dr. Tyler did not identify the specific causes of such decline, the level of collaboration among members of an institution is one of the primary factors involved. As faculty withdraw—both from each other and from the administrative demands they grow to resent—creative work diminishes, and the intellectual energy that is actually the organization's lifeblood gradually leaks out as leaders wonder what kind of first aid to administer. Tyler was pleading with those at NTID to take measures that would help them avoid a pattern that he had repeatedly witnessed. Although he did not use these words, Tyler was calling for members of the organization to be generative and provident at the same moment.

A generative person or organization embraces ideas that give birth to other ideas. John Goodlad's associates program gave birth to a similar program in our own partnership. The National Network for Educational Renewal (NNER) itself, as well as Goodlad's Center for Educational Renewal, have been supportive organizations to collaborative initiatives throughout the nation and models for others to follow as they redesign their own institutional structures devoted to educational change. The wetlands program mentioned earlier helped give rise to the National Science Foundation (NSF) project, and then the NSF project helped the wetlands program expand its influence through curriculum development and teacher awareness.

As we review the effective projects that have been sponsored by our partnership, we conclude that each one is generative in some way. Such projects continually yield greater results than the project leaders initially imagine. This generative spirit was what Ralph Tyler was calling for from the faculty and staff at NTID. He knew that without such a spirit, the institution would eventually forfeit its opportunity to make enduring improvement in the education of deaf students. He was in essence pleading for members of the institution to remember the importance of continually giving their gifts in ways that would lead to others giving. These are the ingredients of the intellectual energy he was espousing.

But even as he spoke there were likely some who were thinking, "Hey wait a minute, I've got a life outside this institution, you know. I can't just devote everything to this place." We all tend to think of our own limitations—particularly the restrictions on our time—and conclude that we are already doing as much as we can do, "so please don't ask me to do any more." This is why the idea of generative planning is so important. Generative planning means that collaborators think early about how one idea might lead to another, how one expenditure of time might actually save time in another way.

This brings us to the notion of providence. A provident planner is one who considers the future and makes provisions for it. The unprovident planner, on the other hand, thinks only of today's resources, today's objective, without looking through the eyepiece of the telescope that shows the distant scene—the needs of those who will come after us. Tyler was actually asking faculty and staff to do both: to be generative and provident. His comments had implications for hiring practices, administrative style, and institutional structure, as well as for funding patterns—all the issues that institutions engage in daily but are seldom reviewed with an eye on the future.

In one sense, all that occurs in collaborative renewal should be done providentially. Educators are working to improve learning for current students so that the children of these students will benefit. Teacher educators are working to provide a stronger corps of teachers so that future generations will be taught more effectively. All of education is an act of providence. And if collaborators plan with the future in mind, if they create programs that give rise to even stronger programs, and if they consider the long-term needs of those they serve, then they will find balance in the planning process. They will achieve a disciplined openness that will permit their organizations to grow in ways that will edify current students, as well as students who will come to them in the future.

Key #7

Transformative
Evaluation

A s a young faculty member, the first author was asked by a dean
of another college to evaluate an undergraduate course. "I'm
getting too many complaints from students about this course," the
dean admitted. "Many of our sections have over 300 students, and
even with a graduate assistant's help, we're not giving students what
they need. I know we can do better."

As an external evaluator, I designed a questionnaire, piloted it
with a small group of students, and then administered it to a large
sample of students who had recently taken the course. I also interviewed every faculty member who taught the course, as well as the
graduate assistants who worked with students in weekly help sessions. As the results came in, I was concerned about how I was going
to break the news to the department that its course was one of the
least appreciated on campus. On the questionnaire item that asked
students to compare this course with others they had completed at
the university, over half responded that it was worse than most or
one of the worst. In general, students saw the course lectures as

ineffective and the help sessions led by graduate assistants as the course's saving grace.

When I presented the data to the department, one faculty member said, "Maybe we should eliminate the graduate students from the course." Thinking that he had misread the data, I again placed a transparency on the overhead projector and said, "These items show that the graduate assistants are viewed by students as the most valuable part of the course." Without hesitating, he argued, "But maybe the students like the grad assistants for the wrong reasons."

At this point, I was unsure how to proceed. Obviously, faculty who were teaching the course were not interpreting the data as I was, and certainly not coming to the same conclusions about how the course should be improved. Although the study was defensible from the standpoint of traditional evaluation criteria, I did not believe that it would actually result in an improved course. This evaluation suffered from a dual imposition: The dean mandated it, and an external evaluator unknown to the professors executed it. In addition, the professors were teaching the same course without consulting with each other about content or pedagogy. There was almost no real collaboration occurring. So although one professor might have gained some insight from the data, there was no assurance that others would benefit from the insight.

The Evaluation Tension

Any change initiative brings with it tensions related to evaluation. Parents, teachers, students, and administrators all need to know whether the new approach is better than the old one. In collaborative change, the tension takes on unique dimensions because the emphasis is on relationships and creativity. Neither of these aspects was present in the course evaluation just recounted. Professors were cordial, but they seldom spoke to one another about the course they were all teaching. And most were more concerned about maintaining the course than they were about creating something that would better serve students' needs.

Those involved in collaborative renewal are interested both in the well-being of each other and in the interests of their students.

Evaluations mandated by an administrator or the state might be of some value to collaborators, but such studies will never provide the kind of information participants need to keep the renewal process alive. In collaborative educational renewal, evaluation must not be viewed as something one must do to satisfy a decision maker or an outside constituency. The evaluation must become an integral part of the renewal process itself.

Collaborators who see the partnership effort primarily from the viewpoint of relationships will typically emphasize the importance of *process evaluation*—gathering data on the collaborative act itself. We frequently engaged in this type of evaluation in the early stages of our partnership. Several studies at that time documented the nature of the partnership, the organizational structures that were developed to sustain the effort, and the activities in which partners engaged. Process evaluators are not so concerned with how much improvement is taking place due to a certain activity, but focus rather on the quality of the interaction that surrounded the activity.

Those who are more results oriented want to gather data to determine the effects of collaborative work on the students the partnership has been designed to serve. These participants value *outcome evaluation*. They argue that no matter how much people might like each other, the only question worth posing is, "Are students benefiting from all this collaborative work, and, if so, what kinds of benefits are they experiencing?" If a new teacher education program is implemented, the outcome evaluators want to know whether those trained in the new program are more or less effective than those prepared in the former program. If a new approach to literacy education is introduced, they want to know if the reading level of children has improved as a result.

When the outcome people and the process people come together in the same meeting, the discussion can become heated. The process advocates accuse the outcome proponents of pushing too fast for too much, and the outcome people accuse the process participants of being too soft on what really matters. Like other tensions, this one can either strengthen or weaken the collaborative change effort. If the process people win, participants will never be able to understand the effects of their initiatives; if the outcome people win, collaborative relationships will be strained and the partnership could eventually dissolve.

Balancing Evaluation Tensions

If the outcome process tensions are to be resolved, participants must emphasize mutuality in their relationships and gift giving in their approach to creative work—the foundational elements of renewal. We call the balance point between the two poles *transformative evaluation*. Whereas educational partnerships have promoted collaborative research and inquiry—a type of scholarly investigation that is changing the very nature of scholarship in education—collaborative forms of evaluation have seldom been addressed in the education literature (see Osguthorpe, 1996a).

In collaborative research, school and university educators join together to pursue common questions that arise out of classroom practice (see Cochran-Smith, 1993; Sergiovanni, 1996), with the goal of improving teaching and learning. How, then, do educators collaboratively assess the worth of an educational intervention in ways that lead to transformation? Who determines which data will be collected and by whom? How are data shared with the stakeholders?

Although Sirotnik (1994) and Clark (1995) address the importance of evaluating the school as a whole, and Stake (1995) describes a method of data collection that can treat the whole school as a *case*, no one describes evaluation as a transformative process. It stands to reason, however, that if collaboration among stakeholders is the central feature of educational partnerships, new approaches to evaluation must be developed just as new approaches to research and inquiry have emerged that fit the new environments of partner schools and centers of pedagogy.

Elements of Transformative Evaluation

By placing the prefix *trans* before the common designation *formative*, we emphasize the role of evaluation in collaborative change. *Transform* literally means to change forms or structures, to go through a metamorphosis. In collaborative renewal, the *transforming* process must be experienced by all involved in the evaluation—by those who pose the questions, as well as by those who gather data to answer them. Evaluation that transforms is evaluation that leads to personal as well as organizational renewal because collaborators are literally feeding each other what they need to keep growing and changing.

Because it is a continual process, transformative evaluation is often indistinguishable from other collaborative work. The questions that lead to transformation come naturally and frequently as collaborators attempt to improve their practice. Although formal publication is not the primary aim of this type of evaluative work, documenting progress is essential. If asked to identify areas for professional development, most experienced teachers will express a need to improve their writing skills. They are not so much interested in formal publication—as are university faculty—but in the prospect of documenting their growth, sharing ideas with other teachers, and refining their ideas by writing about them.

Transformative evaluation leads not only to professional growth and program improvement, but often to changes in the evaluation approach itself. The methods and strategies for evaluation are not always predetermined, but may be allowed to unfold as the change process dictates. Collaborative renewal means that the change process—including the evaluation—is always up for review. Participants are not compelled to hold rigidly to one evaluation model or another, but base their methodology decisions on the needs of those engaging in the initiative. Thus, rather than being viewed as an intruder or an interruption to the change process, transformative evaluation is seen by participants as a friend.

A Partner School as a Case of Collaborative Evaluation

One partner school in the BYU-Public School Partnership has been experimenting the past 2 years with transformative evaluation. As the new elementary teacher education program was designed and implemented in the fall of 1994, all stakeholders agreed that the program would need careful evaluation to determine whether it should be continued and expanded to other partner schools. Because the program required that students preparing to be teachers spend 2 full years in a partner school and that pedagogy courses be taught in the school rather than at the university, an approach to evaluation was needed that would capitalize on the increased collaboration that was occurring in the school. Teachers, professors, and students agreed to participate together in evaluating the new program. Evaluation teams were formed, and data were collected. Some might view some of the methods as participant observation or action research because evaluators included teachers and professors who were themselves part of the intervention.

As the first year of the program progressed, a consultant from the partnership helped teachers form inquiry groups that began pursuing pedagogical questions they felt the school needed to investigate (see Herrmann et al., 1996). A BYU student researcher also conducted observations of classroom practice under the joint direction of a professor and the assistant principal (Barfuss, 1996). The year-long multifaceted evaluation, including the collaborative inquiry groups and the student observations, changed the nature of research and evaluation in this partner school. These activities had a transforming effect not only on programs but on participants as well.

We have identified five characteristics of transformative evaluation that we believe are essential to collaborative renewal. We call them "the five I's" of transformative evaluation: 1) interactive, 2) internally initiated, 3) integrated, 4) informative, and 5) inexpensive. By evaluating collaborative change with approaches that include these characteristics, educators will balance the tensions associated with evaluation.

Foster Evaluative Interaction

Some of the good conversation in which collaborators engage will focus on evaluating the change that is being implemented. Evaluation is interactive, as educators jointly determine the goals, the design, the data collection and analysis procedures, and the results. Unlike some forms of evaluation where the evaluators must remain distant from those being evaluated, transformative evaluation demands that participants—those involved most intimately in the intervention—contribute to every phase of the evaluation.

For evaluative interaction to occur, participants must have already developed relationships of mutuality and be seeking thresholds to change. Their purpose for engaging in such dialogue is to identify ways to improve. All participants welcome comments from others that will help them discover a new approach to a problem they have been trying to solve. As coworkers share ideas for identifying these thresholds, they are entering into the gift giving described earlier in this book. Rather than viewing evaluation as painful or wasteful, participants see it as a way of offering to each other suggestions that will strengthen their combined efforts.

Initiate Inside-Out Evaluations

Most evaluation is conducted because a decision maker requests information, just as the dean described earlier requested the study of the undergraduate course. But in transformative evaluation, stakeholders must feel the need to gather data before an evaluation is planned; the evaluation must be *internally initiated*. Traditional evaluation is built around what Hyde (1983) calls the "market exchange" model, a model that is motivated from outside the organization (p. 114). An evaluator is invited to submit a proposal to respond to questions the decision makers wish to answer. A contract is then forged between the buyer (the decision makers) and the seller (the evaluator). If either party reneges on the contract, each has a right to make demands on the other.

In such evaluation, the evaluator takes on the characteristics of a merchant selling a service and, like a merchant in former societies, often feels like a foreigner—one who is outside the tribe being evaluated. The objectivist approach assumes that data will be interpreted more accurately when the evaluator is a stranger. When participants see evaluation as something they naturally do to help one another improve, however, the market exchange approach loses its power. Like members of families, collaborators who have developed relationships of mutuality are able to offer more valuable suggestions to each other for strengthening their individual contributions than those outside the inner circle.

When evaluation is initiated from inside the organization, data take on more value and have the potential to effect meaningful change. Inside-out evaluations are not limited to insiders as data sources or as the interpreters of results. An internally initiated evaluation might involve those external to the organization, but such contributors are invited to participate by those who are most deeply involved in the renewal effort itself, rather than by a person or agency with only distant connections.

Integrate Evaluation
Into the Organization

Rather than viewing evaluation as an appendage to partner school work, participants must come to view evaluation as an essential, integrated aspect of the school itself. Evaluation becomes part of the continuing conversation regarding partner school activities rather than an afterthought. When new programs are planned, evaluation is naturally considered at the outset and becomes woven into every phase of the development of the intervention. Critically assessing the worth of each classroom and school practice becomes one aspect of the ethos of the partner school.

Participants can recognize that evaluation has become integral to their work when they no longer associate it only with formal studies. In collaborative change, participants may conduct surveys, analyze achievement test scores, or develop interview schedules for teachers or students. But these more formal efforts will not be seen as the heart of the evaluative process. Rather, those involved will continually be judging the worth of their efforts. In uncomplicated ways, they will articulate needs as they arise—needs that propel rather than impede the change process. Such judgments will be offered to others not as formative or summative decisions but as transformative gifts that lead to enduring change in the organization.

The teachers who asked the university to reconsider its graduate offerings in light of the needs of practicing professionals were in reality offering evaluative data to their partner institution. They were saying in essence, "We want to experience professional development, but your current programs do not seem to meet our needs. They are too narrow, too specialized to be of much help to us in our everyday teaching." Some might have labeled their remarks as summative data that could lead to the dissolution of current programs. Others might have seen their comments as formative data that university personnel could use to improve existing programs. We choose to view their contribution as transformative. Partly because of the teachers' willingness to offer their opinion, the university is currently reviewing its master's programs and considering a cross-departmental offering that would respond more effectively to the needs of classroom teachers.

Communicate With
Benevolence and Honesty

Because transformative evaluation is intimately connected with the people and practices in a partner school, it is more informative to stakeholders than evaluation that is objectively detached. And when data are informative, educators will ensure that the appropriate questions are posed and data are gathered. The kind of communication that develops in collaborative educational renewal is a benevolent honesty. Most leaders today believe that being unmistakably clear in communication is important. But clarity, we believe, is not enough. One can be clear without being honest. And one can be clear without being kind.

Collaborative renewal requires that participants be both benevolent and honest. Without benevolence, relationships may be strained to the point that the collaborative effort is destroyed. Without honesty, the creative act is diminished. If a product of the change process is not of high quality, participants need to express themselves. But unlike organizations with low levels of collaboration, an expression of concern is not adequate because it is not transformative by itself. If collaborative renewal is to occur, those communicating a concern need to offer more than simple off-handed criticism: They need to offer their help to improve the product. In this way, transformative evaluation goes further than other types of evaluation because it causes participants to move beyond data to the intervention being addressed.

Reduce Evaluation Expenses

Transformative evaluation is inexpensive because it is a natural part of the change process. There are no contracts, no major funding decisions. Granted, professional time and supplies are devoted to the process, but there is no reason to place these expenditures on a separate budget line because the activities are indistinguishable from other aspects of collaborative renewal. Participants who engage in transformative evaluation are sharing information every day. Expecting them to keep track of how much time was devoted to evaluative conversation would be counterproductive.

We recognize that most collaboratives must begin by hiring evaluation consultants to assist participants in establishing a culture that welcomes evaluation activities. In the early stages, such a consultant may need to supervise a corps of assistants who gather data of various sorts for collaborators' use. But as the effort matures, participants themselves should become the data gatherers: the posers of questions that need to be answered for the change process to succeed. These lower costs for evaluation do not occur because leaders decide to reallocate the budget. The cost reduction gradually accrues because evaluation becomes a natural function of all participants.

Key #8

Parity

In the early stages of our partnership, a conference was held for all school and university educators. In one of the sessions, an assistant principal from a junior high school stood and said, "I like the partnership. It's given us a lot of opportunities at our school that we wouldn't have had otherwise, but I'm worried that we're contributing much more than we're getting in return." In the following session, a university professor who was unaware of the assistant principal's comment, expressed the flip side: "The partnership has potential, but it seems to me like it's a one-way street—all the resources are flowing from the university to the schools, and very little is coming back to us." Both of these partners were grappling with the *giving and receiving* tension. Both felt somehow that they had been short-changed, that they had given more than they had received.

Because collaborative work relies primarily on giving time and effort rather than money, partners often avoid discussing the relative merits of each one's contribution. Without a ledger sheet that can be reviewed by an accountant, participants often feel confused about the relative nature of each partner's effort compared with the rewards each receives for active involvement. If this confusion develops, participants may not wish to discuss the tension, fearing that others will see them as being selfish or as detracting from collaborative work. But the tension will likely surface at some point, as it did with the assistant principal and university faculty member.

The giving-receiving tension, as shown in Table 1 (p. xx, this volume) has two poles: uniformity and diversity. If partners slide too far to the uniformity side, they begin calling for sameness in contribution and rewards. The assistant principal, for example, might have argued that for every hour spent by his faculty in the supervision of student teachers, university faculty should contribute 1 hour to his school. Pulling too far in this direction will usually alienate certain partners, because if pressed beyond their ability to give, they will simply stop participating. Many in a partnership move to this side of the tension, however, because they feel that it will more tightly define the nature of their collaborative work and bring greater definition to the benefits each partner can expect to receive.

On the subjective side of the tension, partners recognize the futility of trying to force each other to make uniform contributions. They believe that because partners are qualitatively different, each will make a unique contribution, and any attempt to quantify contributions can potentially damage relationships and hence the viability of the organization as a whole. Rather than arguing that each partner contribute exactly the same time and effort, they emphasize diversity of contribution and rewards. These collaborators might say, "Let's just accept the fact that we're going to get less from this than we're putting in." If participants pull too far in this direction, the collaborative endeavor loses its focus on a common set of goals, and participants become disillusioned.

To define the balance point between the extremes of uniformity and diversity, we use the term *parity*. We have seen partnerships that emphasize uniformity or diversity in their early stages of development, but to endure, any collaborative organization will eventually need to arrive at a position of parity. Parity does not imply that two things are exactly the same, just that they are equivalent or similar in value. The power of the term comes from how this similarity is determined. Whether one is dealing with equivalency in monetary currencies or in the "evenness" of two political principles, parity is determined by common consent of the people. No one can decide unilaterally that the French franc is worth 10 dollars. Value in international monetary markets is jointly determined, just as the worth of collaborative contributions is jointly determined by the participants.

But the connotations of the term *parity* extend beyond its traditional meaning of comparative valuing. The term can also include the notions of reciprocity and joint possession. In collaborative educational renewal, partners reciprocate without paying attention to the relative size of each other's contribution. They move beyond the assistant principal and faculty member who felt short-changed because they come to see themselves as givers and receivers of gifts—gifts that come to be viewed by all participants as joint possessions. When partners begin to view their work and contributions in this way, no one will feel short-changed.

Parity is thus a condition of balanced creative contribution, a circumstance in which all participants thoughtfully give and graciously receive. Those who pull too far in the direction of diversity are not as thoughtful of their partner as they might be, and those who pull too far in the direction of uniformity are not as gracious as one would hope. And if grace and thought slowly trickle out of collaborative work, personal and professional renewal will gradually evaporate.

When parity exists, partners take joint possession of the results of their work without consciously analyzing their efforts. The common goals do not need to be rehearsed, because each participant has already internalized them. Participants' evaluation activities have transformed them and their work: focusing them on the task at hand, protecting them from unproductive diversions that could keep them from renewing teaching and learning.

Although many of the other keys to collaborative renewal can be achieved by following certain steps, parity seems to be a condition that emerges on its own. Each pole suggests several "thou shalt nots," but the balance point itself is less achievable by direct means. Partners gradually can become better at recognizing it and fostering it, but they cannot create it by following three easy procedures. In fact, for parity to exist, balance must first be achieved on each of the other seven tensions. Thus, parity is an overarching balance point, a state of mind, a condition of the heart that affects and is affected by each of the other seven keys to collaborative renewal. Before experiencing parity, a collaborative must establish the balance points of qualified membership, role flexibility, interdependence, nurtured development, disciplined openness, and transformative evaluation.

Although parity will naturally emerge as participants find the balance point on each of the other seven tensions, our experience suggests three ways to recognize and foster it in a collaborative organization: 1) emphasize equivalence, 2) nurture reciprocal respect, and 3) jointly possess the goods of accomplishment.

Emphasize Equivalence

We are acquainted with collaborative initiatives that function more like corporations than like educational partnerships. Rather than contributing time and talents to achieve common goals, these organizations attempt to measure every effort in dollars and cents. University faculty who conduct professional development seminars in partner school districts are paid at the usual consulting rate. Teachers in the district who help supervise student teachers work through their unions to demand adequate reimbursement for their time. The relationship is very clear and simple: Every hour that is contributed to the collaborative should be compensated appropriately by the partner receiving the benefit.

We do not believe that such organizations lead to collaborative renewal. Although they might serve the needs of current students to some extent, they do not provide for continuing growth of all participants. To experience renewal, partners must emphasize equivalence rather than sameness—equity rather than equality. When collaboratives function in this way, they seldom equate effort with money, but look at the relative worth to each organization of each partner's contribution.

When collaborators emphasize equivalence, they realize that participants' contributions may be quite dissimilar during a single phase, but will even out over time. The 4th-grade teacher who feels that she has given too many extra hours to a math education project may later be released from teaching for 1 year to help supervise teachers in the implementation of the new curriculum. A university faculty member whose teaching assignment has left no room for research may later be given time to collaborate with school faculty on classroom research that will lead to an improved supervision model. The point is that partners offer to each other changes in roles and assignments that lead to professional growth, as well as to school renewal.

In these examples, educators are not counting the hours they are contributing to a particular cause—they are simply working together for a common goal, assuming that the goodwill of their partner will lead to a parity. Partners discuss frequently the progress of a given initiative, the effectiveness of each contributor's efforts, and possible changes in future directions. But those involved recognize that each participant offers something unique to the overall effectiveness of the joint effort, and that forcing partners to make identical contributions would only lower the probability of success. Thus, they emphasize equivalence of contribution and expect that equity and fairness will prevail in due time.

Nurture Reciprocal Respect

Parity can be achieved only if partners develop respect for one another. One meaning of the word *parity* is that two groups evenly esteem each other. When this evenness of esteem does not exist, groups usually develop prejudices toward one another. As Young-Bruehl (1996) explains in *The Anatomy of Prejudices*:

> Groups that have common goals and are "positively interde-pendent" do not hate and stigmatize each other, while groups that are vying for dominance or competing with each other develop derogatory attitudes that explain their animosity. This theory implies that dominant groups develop prejudices that function to keep their subordinates in place. Their prejudices increase when they feel threatened, when the subordinates seem to be engaging in either rebellion or increased competition. Allies or partners do not need prejudices: negative prejudices do not exist among equals. (p. 50)

One would not normally associate respect with a tension that we have labeled *giving and receiving*. We have found, however, that the attitudes that partners hold toward one another are more powerful determinants of renewal than the specific wording of a goal or the process used to account for time and effort. If one traces the history of the relationship between schools and universities—or between any two unlike partners—one usually discovers a certain amount of prejudice. One group often tries to dominate the other, devaluing the

other's ability to contribute to any common goal. "University professors just don't understand the world of practice," or "Teachers in the
schools just don't understand the latest educational research." Such
comments develop anything but parity. They feed negative stereo-
types that lock old prejudices in place and keep unhealthy competi-
tion alive.

Relationships of mutuality are the antithesis of prejudice, and to
build on these relationships, partners must continually hold a high
level of respect for each other. One teacher educator in our partnership has developed such high respect for an elementary school
teacher that on their first day of class each semester, she takes her
cohort of university students to this teacher's classroom to observe
her at work. The faculty member explains that "after watching this
teacher for just 1 hour, my students are inspired to aim higher, to be
the best teachers they can possibly be."

Reciprocal respect must occur not only between partners but
within each individual organization. A university faculty member
who was concerned about a recent internal program review said, "We
don't need any more budget from the administration. We are not even
asking for higher salaries. We just need to know that our contribution
is valued. We just want a little respect." School educators often have
similar feelings. They need to know that administrators and other
educators in the district value their accomplishments and respect
them for the contribution they are making. Although many may not
directly express it, they view this type of respect as a direct benefit of
collaborative work, and the lack of respect as a direct cost—a drain
on their ability to contribute.

When collaborative renewal is occurring, partners will automat-
ically offer respect to one another. They will come to value the
uniquely different skills of other participants, and in the process they
will become both givers and receivers of esteem. This form of reciprocity is expressed best in the Quaker proverb "It is the not-me in
thee that is to me most precious" (cited by Young-Bruehl, 1996, p. 1).

Jointly Possess the
Goods of Accomplishment

As central as respect is to the process of parity, it is not enough.
Kenneth Strike (1990) asserts that both the "goods of accomplish-

ment" and the "goods of relationship" are part of the ethics of teaching—the requirements for improving educational practice (p. 216). Collaborative educational renewal will always yield goods of accomplishment. If such goods are not coming from cooperative effort, renewal is by definition not occurring. These goods may not always be readily recognized. They may be as tangible as a new set of curriculum materials, or as illusive as lower dropout rates or higher levels of teacher satisfaction. But if renewal is actually occurring, some type of "goods" will result.

When parity exists, partners take joint possession of the goods of accomplishment. They avoid comparing "ledger sheets," partly because their common agenda drives their work and partly because collaboration as gift giving precludes comparisons. As participants experience transformative gift giving, their approaches to learning and teaching change. The success of their partner is as fulfilling as their own success because each one possesses the success: The school principal who describes the master's program in educational leadership as "*our* principal preparation program," or the high school English teacher who says, "*We* really need to take another look at the way *we* help university students develop classroom management skills." In both cases, school educators view university programs as theirs. They no longer see their contributions as benefiting only the university, but come to view them as direct benefits of their work in the schools. Likewise, university faculty who work closely with teachers in the schools begin to see issues that face the school as their issues. If the state mandates a change in curriculum that is viewed as ineffective, university faculty join with the schools in their attempts to revise the mandate or respond to it in a way that will benefit the children and youth who come within their stewardship.

Summary

In this section of the book, we have described five tensions that surround the creative process associated with collaborative renewal: 1) planning, 2) approach to change, 3) amount of change, 4) evaluation, and 5) giving and receiving. Each of these tensions has two poles that must be addressed continually if balance is to be found and the change process is to succeed. When each of the poles is considered and measures are taken to balance them, participants will recognize and cross thresholds that lead to creative educational change. There are five keys to finding such balance: 1) nurtured development, 2) inquiring change agentry, 3) disciplined openness, 4) transformative evaluation, and 5) parity. When these keys are used, the tensions that normally arise in collaborative work will become positive ingredients rather than frustrating inhibitors of the change process.

We began this section of the book by discussing how participants in collaborative initiatives can recognize the thresholds that will lead to creative change. These thresholds are the primary ingredients of collaborative renewal, and when partners fail to recognize or cross the thresholds, renewal will cease. In the final chapter of the book, we will show how the tensions we have introduced relate to other ways of looking at collaborative change, and how those viewpoints can help educators gain new perspectives on their efforts to improve learning and teaching.

Partnering: Adventures and Analogies

Forming, sustaining, and expanding a partnership is a matter of creating a new culture. New roles must be learned; different values must be sustained. Time is required to build relationships, lay foundations, make decisions, and assure that all participants have opportunities to give unselfishly and receive gracefully. This requires patience and persistence. Participants can be easily turned away from the new culture when their needs do not seem to be met and their contributions do not seem adequately valued. When these individuals develop a spirit of mutuality and collaboration with their colleagues, however, when partners become fully engaged in mutually beneficial efforts at renewal, and when partners are willing to take appropriate risks and commit to appropriate change, partnership can become a joyful adventure.

The BYU-Public School Partnership has been in operation for roughly 14 years. Today its agenda embraces a rich array of activities, including hundreds of school and university personnel. Although both the capacity and the extent of current activities would seem to indicate considerable stability and hardiness, there is still reason to look critically at our culture. Each time key people need to be replaced, we as participants feel uncertain as to whether the culture of partnering will continue to grow or flourish. As the agenda expands to include new and bigger projects, it is easy to wonder whether or not the demands of growth will be too great. Ours is a struggle of constantly addressing issues related to sustaining the partnership culture. We are anxious to show some of the insight we have gained from our adventure.

There is much rhetoric advocating and supporting school-university partnerships, and it has grown significantly during the last decade. The popularity of the partnership principle for organizing and conducting the operations of preparing teachers and renewing schools is readily visible. As the rhetoric and advocacy increase, more and more schools and universities are labeling themselves *partnerships*. The label may be readily claimed; the rhetoric may be expressed with relative ease. But the successful development and operation of a partnership is a much more difficult matter.

After years of experience in trying to build, sustain, and enrich school-university partnerships, we have concluded that far more attention needs to be directed to the practical, day-to-day "in the trenches" operations than currently exists. This discussion of tensions and points of balance is an effort to look inside the workings of partnerships.

In Part I, we note the observation of a colleague who described a partnership as "an unnatural act among consenting adults." Behind the humor, there is keen insight and understanding within the statement. We devote Part I to examining the relationships of mutuality that are not always natural but can become highly beneficial if that consenting includes willingness to embrace a varied membership and balance the tensions resulting from that variety; accepting the risks and effort involved in developing interdependence; and remaining flexible where positions, roles, viewpoints, and power are concerned. In Part II, we examine gifts that partners give and receive in the process of collaboration: gifts of creativity, teaching, nurturing, validation, and transformative evaluation.

Analogy I:
Partnership as an Adventure

James Rowley (1988) offers a useful metaphor for the teaching-learning experience, a metaphor we earlier linked to our perceptions of partnership and cultural change: Drawing from his own experiences in leading students on canoe outings in the wilderness, he identifies four outcomes of such an adventure that he feels capture the essence of positive learning environments: cooperation, involvement, risk taking, and association. These outcomes are relevant to the partnership effort; they offer many insights concerning needs, tensions, and causal relationships with which our partnership has been involved.

Cooperation

First, Rowley (1988) emphasizes the importance of developing a spirit of cooperation among the participants. Often, young people do not join a wilderness experience with an inclination to cooperate. Some see the trip as an opportunity to compete or to excel, an occasion to show their great strength, ability, or knowledge. They seek to win and to gain recognition. Others attempt to avoid competing with or showing off to their peers. They isolate themselves and seek personal goals, with very limited need for or interest in their colleagues. But at some point in the experience, the participants are awakened to the need for and value of working together. Rowley asserts that his best outdoor adventure experiences have been those on which a strong cooperative spirit has developed. He comments:

> These groups [which developed a cooperative spirit] seemed to be hungrier for new knowledge and skills and demonstrated an ability to master them more easily. Perhaps more important, the individual members of such groups seemed to feel better about themselves and the people with whom they had shared the experience. (p. 14)

Shifting from his outdoor experiences to his professional experiences as an educator working with colleagues, Rowley (1988) concludes, "The best years of my career were those where I was involved in working cooperatively with colleagues" (p. 14). He applies this insight specifically to teacher education by observing, "The design of new programs in teacher preparation must seek to create opportunities for prospective teachers to develop the skills and attitude necessary to create and maintain professional relationships based on collaboration and collegiality" (p. 14).

Rowley's (1988) comments are particularly applicable to public school-university partnerships, because working cooperatively extends to a wide variety of colleagues and person-centered programs, for prospective teachers are generally a product of such partnerships. Both school and university people tend to work somewhat in isolation within the confines of their classrooms, offices, or laboratories. For these individuals, the idea of opening their doors to others—not just cooperating with an occasional favor but collaborating by sharing creation and ownership of professional products—can be a formidable and often daunting challenge. It disrupts comfort zones, it requires changes in behaviors, and it often consumes extra time. Frustrations inevitably surface, as participants quickly realize that it would be easier to work alone or to work with a limited, carefully selected group of team members who are much alike. Like those teenagers who are anxious to prove themselves the strongest and the best at the expense of their associates, some fear that admitting others into their spotlight would force them to share it. Like the wilderness participants who prefer to pursue their own interests in their own way, others simply do not want interference in their pet projects or ideas. But like the young people in Rowley's experience, those who come to recognize the value of two paddlers in a rowboat benefit from each other's strength.

Involvement

A second aspect of Rowley's (1988) metaphor of adventure stresses that adventure frequently requires high levels of involvement. Considerable physical, mental, and emotional energy is expended in wilderness survival. Participants are constantly challenged to meet new expectations and embrace new opportunities, often with the necessity of using new knowledge and skills. Drawing from the work of Czikszentmihalyi, Rowley points out that "the good guide understands the importance of creating a learning environment where there is a balance between newly acquired knowledge and skills and the real life challenges against which they are tested" (p. 14). In an ideal circumstance, the experience is difficult enough to challenge the participants, but not so demanding that it is beyond their ability. Rowley further relies on Czikszentmihalyi to conclude that "the challenges confronted [must be] real as well as appropriate to the skills, knowledge, and attitudes of the participant" (p. 14)

Rowley's (1988) comments bring to mind a group of elementary teachers we described in an earlier chapter. Seven or eight teachers came to the partnership requesting an opportunity to work on graduate degrees based on research they would conduct on topics relevant to their classrooms, with credit for projects that would implement their research for the benefit of their students. One of the teachers described her personal struggle with the desire for knowledge and skills:

> I stand on the cusp of this new age, and I feel challenged to meet the needs of my students. I have seen the dynamics of children, teaching, and the world change. I want so many things for my personal practice. I have weathered enough storms to have deep questions emerging from my practice: "How do you educate children for the 21st century?" (Lynette Christian, personal communication, April 11, 1997)

Through the partnership, these teachers were able to undertake a program that would enable them to explore the areas they found important in their practice. One of the teachers was interested in helping children with attention deficit disorder; another wanted to find ways of incorporating inquiry into her curriculum. Through the partnership, a meeting was set up for these teachers with the dean and associate dean of our school of education. A program is being developed, and these teachers are increasing their knowledge and skills with research and projects based in the place they feel safest and most competent: their own classrooms. Involvement, opportunity, and safety have all been provided through this partnership project.

Risk Taking

Risk, with the dissonance that tends to accompany it, is the third element Rowley (1988) identifies in his analogy of adventure. When individuals are faced with situations where they are called on to learn and use new skills or to apply and test old skills in new and challenging ways, they sense the possibility of failure, and with it a degree of unease or discomfort. Of course, when individuals face these conditions and manage to succeed, their fears, apprehensions, and self-doubt turn into feelings of achievement, satisfaction, and pride. Although misgivings and fears can reach levels of intensity that may be harmful and debilitating, when anticipated and controlled, "they can contribute to creating a productive learning environment where group members feel more excitement than fear, more anticipation than anxiety" (p. 15). Occasionally, a participant may fail to achieve a goal fully but gain sufficient strength and assurance from the partial success to move forward and take on even more demanding requirements.

The point of risk brings to mind another of our partnership adventures mentioned in several earlier chapters: the collaborative restructuring of Brigham Young University's (BYU) elementary teacher preparation program. During the experimental implementation of the program, cohorts of preservice teachers were placed in classrooms in a local elementary school, and teachers from the university traveled to the school to deliver the teaching methods classes on-site. Professors conducted college courses in an elementary classroom, with children running past the door to recess and the band practicing in the room next door. Teachers from the school were invited to attend any classes they desired, so there were times when they found themselves telling their students how to handle children with full-time child handlers sitting on the back row. Some of the professors risked even more as they taught demonstration lessons to the elementary classes—in front of the cohort students and the mentor teacher. All participants were subject to intensive evaluation procedures.

At a meeting of the Elementary Education Department at the close of the first year, one of the administrators referred to the university and school teachers who had participated in the experimental program as "having been through the meat grinder." Risks were taken, crises occurred, people were frustrated, and a few tears were shed. But overall, the risks were something both school and university teachers and administrators could handle. And all were stronger for having handled them.

Association

Rowley's (1988) metaphor of the outdoor adventure begins with cooperation and ends with the bonding that occurs when collaborative relationships become lasting and strong. Adolescents may join a river trip or a survival hike to prove their own strength, to escape from challenges at home, or even to give themselves time and setting to meditate or write. Many begin with such self-interests motivating their participation. But as they share new experiences, laugh together, overcome challenges or adversity, or discover hidden natural beauty, they learn that beneath their diversity are common needs, feelings, emotions, and ideas. They learn to share what is within them, as they discover its worth to others, and they learn in turn to uncover and appreciate what is of worth in their associates. Long after the adventure is over, participants will recall the feelings of closeness they experienced as a group that faced a unique set of problems, persisted in the face of difficulty, and shared expressions of support and encouragement.

One of the most exciting examples of association we have seen in our partnership has been the development of the associates program, described earlier in this book. The 26 people who participated in this program included teachers and administrators from the schools in the five districts making up the partnership, professors from the university's school of education and from arts and sciences departments across the university, and administrators from the state department of education—a disparate group of individuals with a variety of interests and self-interests concerning educational renewal. Modeled on the Leadership Associates Program of the Institute for Educational Inquiry, this series of meetings included several 2-day sessions, held at a resort close to but not within the partnership area, during which assigned readings were explored by participants through a series of discussions and activities.

At first, the presence of the administrators from the state office seemed to be a detriment to the group cohesion. Public school personnel were suspicious of state administrators' interests and motives, and some of the participants made sarcastic remarks about these colleagues. But when group members had shared their feelings and reactions to pertinent education needs—ranging from indignation over gender inequity to tears over the suffering of children—these disparate individuals began to see themselves not merely as individual educators but as members of an education team. One of the public school teachers wrote on her evaluation form, "We've never been treated so well as educators. You made us feel that we were professionals."

Analogy II:
Partnership as Instruments in Tune

As we examine positive outcomes of partnerships, we must also examine the demands that they place on the participants, we applaud the efforts involved in producing the achievements. Like an orchestra comprising many instruments, each with a distinct and significant contribution to an effective performance, a school-university partnership comprises a variety of participants, each with a significant contribution to educational renewal.

Tuning Up

For a violin to produce the desired pitches and tones, the strings must be tuned so they will produce the number of vibrations per second that will result in an *a, e, g,* or *d.* A string that is too taut or too loose will not produce the tone the musician intends. The strings of each instrument must be tuned carefully if the instrument is to contribute its assigned part to the music of the ensemble.

Like each violin in an orchestra, each participant in a partnership needs the proper tension in each string. Too much stress in one area—such as commitment of time, sacrifice of self-interest, or devaluation of one's work or one's specialty area—can produce a tone that is frenzied and sharp. The resulting personal dissonance can make it very difficult for the partner to function optimally in the partnership operation.

When our partnership was engaged in its collaborative effort to restructure the university's elementary education program, many participants found some of their strings wound too tight, and their voices became somewhat shrill. Professors who taught courses in language arts and mathematics became frustrated and taut when professors representing fine arts and physical education claimed that the number of credit hours required in language arts and mathematics should be reduced to allow preservice teachers to have more courses in drama and dance. Public school teachers were tense over the time commitment involved in mentoring large numbers of teacher preparation candidates. They wanted to be sure that their talents and specialties would be recognized and their needs respected. University students who participated in the restructuring meetings tightened everybody's strings when they pointed out that most of the carefully designed curriculum plans would place unfair demands on the students' time.

All participants had years of hard work, sensitive feelings, and personal values at stake in the teacher preparation program. All cared deeply about the education of teachers and children. Such strings normally produce rich music: The tension of caring is vital for the musician or the teacher. But with too much tension, the tones can become dissonant and harsh. Some committee participants complained that their voices were not being heard, as committee chairs complained that discussion was getting out of control. As one committee chair announced with a wry chuckle, "These meetings are going to have to end soon. I'm getting awfully tired of apologizing."

But a good violinist can play in tune on an instrument that is not tuned well. Knowing the music and listening carefully, a skilled musician can make the necessary adaptations to produce accurate pitch and vibrant tone despite a weakness in the instrument. Similarly, skillful and caring educators can adapt their performance to produce rich and harmonious outcomes despite too much tension in one or more areas of their work. As they worked together to restructure the program, our partnership colleagues learned to understand, adapt to, contribute with, and control the weaknesses of their instruments. To ease some of the tension, they laughed together, sang together, and even exercised together. And some tension was important to the performance: It kept the colleagues focused and involved. As a concert violinist once expressed it, "Sharp is sharp, but flat is out of tune." If the tension makes partners a little sharp at times, it is important for us to remember that the common tension of caring is what keeps the effort of the teacher or musician productive and worthwhile.

Playing Together

A solo instrument expresses personal warmth and individuality that is rare in a large ensemble. Solo efforts are important and should be encouraged. But there is a power in the orchestra that comes from a rich blend of varied instruments. When groups of individual instruments—strings, woodwinds, brass, percussion—combine their individual strengths, there are infinite possibilities in the music.

Similarly, the efforts of individual educators are significant and should be encouraged. But the power available in the ensemble of the partnership, like that of the orchestra, comes from individuals within groups combining to focus on purposes, goals, and achievements—and the potentials and possibilities are infinite.

Although the individuals must be aware of the tensions in their own instruments, adapting and controlling so that they can play in tune, those who lead and administer the partnership, like the conductor of the orchestra, must obtain a vision of the final performance and gently guide and instruct each section in making its contribution. Having been in positions analogous to conductor, assistant conductor, or perhaps concertmaster, we suggest a number of areas in which those who conduct might exercise caution in guiding a school-university partnership.

1. *Foster an atmosphere and relationships of trust.* As beginning musicians may be inclined to play softly until they feel comfortable in the ensemble, many participants in partnerships are hesitant to offer their contributions until certain levels of trust have been established. When one of the authors first attended the meetings of the governing board of our partnership, as a recently appointed dean who had come from another university, he did not find it easy to contribute ideas or make comments. The reluctance was largely due to uncertainty he felt in the group. His background was different from that of most partnership participants, some of his ideas were different, and he was not sure how well he or his ideas would be received. Gradually, his feelings have changed. As he has joined with the governing board in resolving a variety of issues, learned quite a bit about board participants, seen evidence of the board members' commitment to partnering as a way of improving education, and developed greater camaraderie with these colleagues, he has been more and more willing to express his ideas, feelings, and reactions.

With each necessary change in the membership of the governing board, the need for trust resurfaces. It is less difficult with the passage of time, however. The group has been meeting almost monthly for 14 years, and a group culture has gradually emerged. All viewpoints are welcomed. No status distinctions exist. Openness and honesty prevail, as do civility and sensitivity. This initial hesitancy of a new board member shows how true sharing and giving may be difficult when positive, supportive relationships have not yet been established. But the ease with which the dean—and other new members—was quickly acclimated shows how a cultural context can communicate expectations, generate trust, and guide relationships as partnerships gain in experience and effectiveness.

2. *Provide a stable organizational structure and strong leadership.* We cannot overemphasize the importance of structure. Members of an orchestra do not sit where they want and play whichever part might interest them. Each player has a place within a section; each section makes a purposeful contribution to the piece of music being performed. Musicians recognize the leadership of their principal, or section leader, and all are attentive to the conductor, who is responsible for interpreting the music and coordinating all efforts into a unified performance. Similarly, in a partnership, the varied participants must look to leaders of sections or units to coordinate unit activities and ultimately to the governing board to coordinate all efforts to accomplish partnership goals. Our governing board, which has met regularly over 14 years to oversee and sustain the workings of the partnership, educates by its very existence. The dean of the school of education and each of the superintendents of the five participating school districts all have equal voting and decision-making power. Procedures are stable and predictable, yet flexible enough to meet continually changing partnership needs. Even though none of the original members remains on the governing board, the group has been expanded, and every position has been filled by two or three different individuals with the passage of time and change of administration, a stable way of relating and doing business has developed that makes it fairly easy for new members to join in and contribute.

Closely related to the need for a stable organizational structure is the need for strong leaders within the system. Their leadership needs to be multifaceted. They must be capable of articulating a vision for partnering, and they must be positioned and disposed to influence others. They do not require titles or impressive lists of administrative responsibilities. It is important that they be people who can recognize problem areas and are capable of offering an informed perspective on them. These leaders are teachers. They help others understand what they are experiencing, and they educate others as to the possibilities and workings of partnerships. Ideally, they need to be proactive in their teaching function: not merely reacting to queries and concerns, but pursuing instructional programs designed to enlarge the base of potential collaborators.

3. *Provide education and training for partnership participants.* An organization without an educational program will eventually weaken and die. In 1995, leaders in our partnership realized that although we had been functioning as a partnership for over a decade, relatively few of those who were influenced by our partnership activities were actually well-informed about and firmly committed to partnership principles. The growth of our partnership's associates program shows our response to the need we feel to educate those who participate in various functions throughout our partnership. This program involves 15 days of meetings and activities designed to promote reflection, expression, understanding, and communication among varied partnership participants. Those 15 days are dispersed throughout the school year, with 2-day retreats alternating with 1-day meetings, activities, and visits to partner schools. The first associates group was so successful that participating members from the state office of education were instrumental in obtaining funding for future programs. The next year two groups conducted regular meetings. Now, during the third year of the program, six groups are in full operation. During this 3-year period, approximately 250 people have been prepared to raise strong voices extending the message of the partnership and to make creative, supportive contributions in partner schools and in partnership projects.

Finale

Whenever people perceive the need for change in something that is important to them, tension will occur. Tension occurs in a teacher who cares for a child struggling to learn to read. When the teacher communicates this tension to a colleague, a principal, a university student, or professor, that tension extends to others who care for the child and for other children who need better programs to meet their literacy needs. The tension in the individual is the beginning of change.

Some tensions develop between individuals as the teacher may investigate new literacy methods and make comments that cause other teachers to be defensive about the methods they have used for many years. Tension may develop if the teacher requests funding, supplies, or release time to search for ways to improve the literacy training of the children in her class. Or tension may occur if the teacher's ideas differ from those that university professors have been teaching the student teachers who are participating at the school. Such tensions may cause discomfort or frustration. But if tensions are controlled by mutual respect among the participants, and if the participants are motivated by a genuine love for the children who are to be affected by the literacy program, these tensions should serve to move rather than to destroy.

In our partnership, many teachers felt tension about the literacy needs of their young students. With an atmosphere of trust and respect in their schools, they felt free to express their tension to their principals, who in turn passed it to the superintendents, who serve on the governing board of the Brigham Young University-Public School Partnership. Literacy has been selected by the governing board as the number-one need for partnership districts at this time, and a plan is now being implemented that will provide all the 500 K-2 teachers in the five districts with professional training in literacy over the next 3- to 4-year period. Literacy faculty at Brigham Young University will participate in the program to ensure that the ideas and practices they present to new teachers entering the profession will be from a perspective compatible with what is being practiced in the schools. Throughout this experience, tension has been felt, but it has been controlled, purposeful, respectful, and positive. Positive tension is an important motivator of commitment, initiative, and renewal.

The purpose of this book has been to represent some roles of positive tensions as they exist in public school-university partnerships. Through our years of partnership activity, we have felt many forms of tension and have generated many as well. We present here what we consider important keys to maximizing the positive effects of tension and reducing the potential damages of tension that is out of control.

Tension—like so many aspects of partnership work, educating, loving, and living—can be a strength or a destroyer, depending on how it is experienced and how it is used. Tension that is selfish and grasping is ultimately destructive, regardless of the extensiveness of programs or the sophistication of partnership structure. Tension that seeks to give and to serve is the tension that brings life and renewal to the individual, the partnership, and the entire community.

From Normal Schools
to Centers of Pedagogy

To gain a greater understanding of the tensions that we identify in this book, one must trace the history of the teaching profession in the United States. One reason the old paradigm of change worked to some extent in 19th-century institutions was due to the self-contained nature of the institutions themselves. *Normal schools,* for example, were organizations that had the authority to dictate both the content and methods portions of the teacher education curriculum. These institutions had little need to develop relationships of mutuality with departments of arts and sciences or with the K-12 schools in the community.

Faculty within normal schools claimed content expertise in the disciplines, as well as the skills needed to direct the laboratory schools where prospective teachers developed the practical ability to function in the profession. In this appendix, we show how the evolution from these self-contained schools to current partner or professional development schools has led to the collaborative approaches we believe are necessary to improve both schooling and teacher education.

The Need for Change

In 1992, the Center for Educational Renewal at the University of Washington conducted a 2-day seminar to promote campuswide commitment to teacher education programs. The seminar grew out of a need identified in a nationwide study of teacher education programs in the United States (see Goodlad, 1990). As the researchers for this study interviewed university faculty and administrators, one conclusion became clear: Most universities that prepare teachers do not place the endeavor as a top priority of the institution, and most arts and sciences faculty see teacher preparation as the responsibility of faculty in education. To counter this isolationist tendency in many institutions, Goodlad requested that, in addition to teacher education and school administrators, arts and sciences administrators attend the seminar.

From our institution, a private university that annually recommends approximately 1,000 graduates for teacher certification, the associate academic vice president of undergraduate programs agreed to attend the seminar. A professor of German and former dean of the College of Humanities, this vice president had had some experience with secondary teacher education majors offered in humanities departments, but had given limited thought to the overall enterprise of teacher preparation and the role of the broader institution in its improvement. Following sessions describing results of the study of teacher education programs, the vice president not only better understood the importance of involving the arts and sciences in teacher preparation programs, but became committed to strengthening such involvement upon his return to campus.

In his subsequent addresses to faculty and administrators in the institution, the vice president called on arts and sciences faculty to contribute more directly to the preparation of teachers:

> I wish that subject-matter departments would join more fully with the College of Education in the preparation of public school teachers. . . . Too often we separate subject matter mastery from learning how to teach. Preparing teachers is a venture in which far more of us should participate. (Britsch, 1992, p. 29)

The following year, he reemphasized his commitment to make teacher education a campuswide endeavor:

Last year I expressed the wish that we would take seriously our responsibility to prepare teachers for the schools. If the efforts of which I have been informed are any indication, we have made real beginnings toward fruitful cooperation during the past months. [These cooperative efforts] raise the hope that we will give up some of the territorial claims that sometimes plague us and think about how we can provide the nation with a corps of teachers who master both their subject matter and the methods of conveying it. (Britsch, 1993, p. 31)

Historical Background

The "territorial claims" that the vice president describes did not develop suddenly on our campus. Like other universities that began as normal schools, the arts and sciences disciplines, as well as other professional programs, gradually established themselves as separate entities, and as they became departments and colleges, they progressively distanced themselves from the preparation of educators. To understand the forces in higher education that led to the separation of "content from pedagogy," one must examine, at least briefly, the history of U.S. institutions that prepare teachers (see Beck, 1980).

Normal Schools

Figure A.1 illustrates the typical organizational structure of the early normal schools established in the 19th century. The dotted lines indicate the connectedness among pedagogy, curriculum content, and the world of practice (the laboratory school) within a single institution. Beginning in the early part of this century, the structure began to change, as illustrated in Figure A.2. Normal schools as such began to disappear as the institutions began to prepare teachers for secondary schools. According to Clifford and Guthrie (1988),

By adding an optional 4-year course, normal schools could train high school teachers along with their traditional elementary school-bound clientele. Despite objections to this trend, based partly on the inadequate training of many of their faculties, eighty-eight state normal schools became teachers colleges between

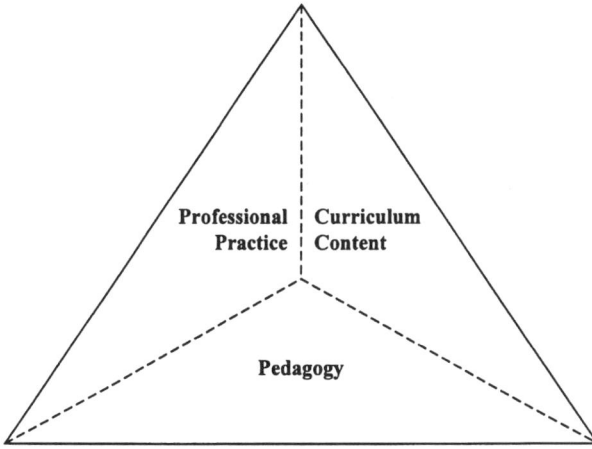

Figure A.1. The Normal School (1823-1910)

1910 and 1930. By 1940 the century-old term *normal school* disappeared into educational history. (p. 60)

Teachers Colleges

As normal schools became teachers colleges, most retained laboratory schools to experiment with pedagogical practice and to pro-

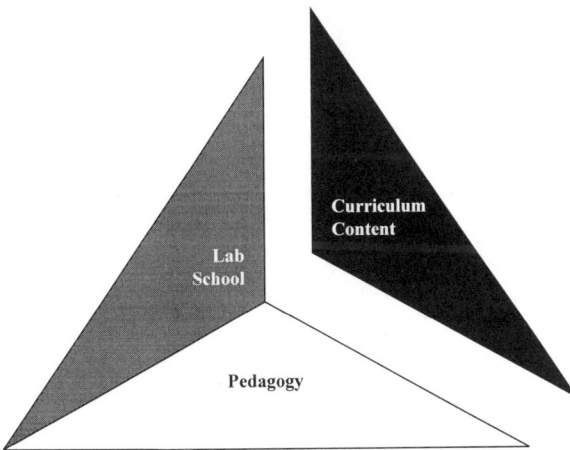

Figure A.2. The Teachers College (1910-1950)

vide settings in which those seeking professional certification could complete their student teaching requirements. As Figure A.2 shows, the curriculum-oriented faculty gradually established its own arts and sciences departments outside the teachers college, and in many cases became the core disciplines in institutions that developed into full-range universities. In some instances, normal schools that became teachers colleges were added to an existing university—often a nearby institution that had a minimum of respect for the normal school because fewer of its faculty generally had obtained advanced degrees.

Beginning in the middle part of the 20th century, many teachers colleges had become schools or colleges of education, and rather than being the central focus of the institution, they were one of many professional or disciplinary emphases a student could pursue. As the arts and sciences became their own distinct organizational units, they began to take increasing responsibility, not only for content education, but also for pedagogical training of their students preparing to be secondary teachers. Thus, while the teachers colleges continued to "own" pedagogical preparation for those preparing to teach in elementary schools, the disciplines gradually assumed responsibility for the preparation of secondary teachers.

As the need for both elementary and secondary teachers continued to grow, laboratory schools could not provide practicum experiences for all the students seeking teacher certification, and so most schools and colleges of education closed their lab schools and began relying on nearby public schools to replace the lab school functions (see Figure A.3).

School-University Partnerships

Although the public schools offered many more classrooms in which to complete education practicum experiences, they often did not provide for the kind of experimentation that most lab schools had attempted to foster. Unlike lab schools, public schools were disconnected from universities by funding structure, administrative control, and organizational mission. These differences often led to awkward and sometimes antagonistic relationships between the universities that were offering courses in teacher education and the schools that were providing settings for students to master needed professional skills. To overcome the problems associated with this physical and psycho-

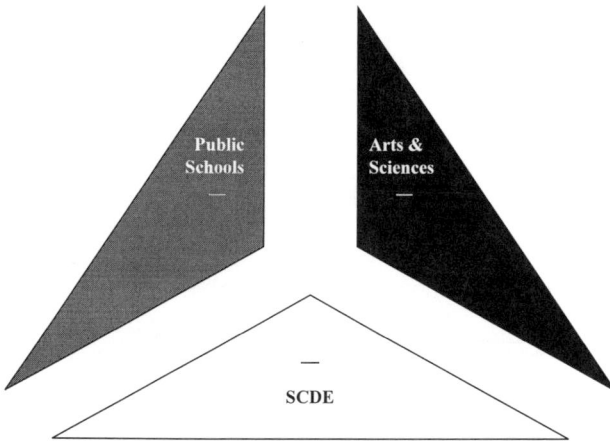

Figure A.3. The School of Education (1950-1980)

logical break between practice and theory, schools and universities began in the 1980s to form partnerships, symbiotic organizations designed to foster the simultaneous improvement of teacher education and schooling (see Goodlad, 1984).

Figure A.4 shows how these early partnerships typically produced effective collaborative relationships between teacher education faculty and public school teachers, but seldom involved departments of arts and

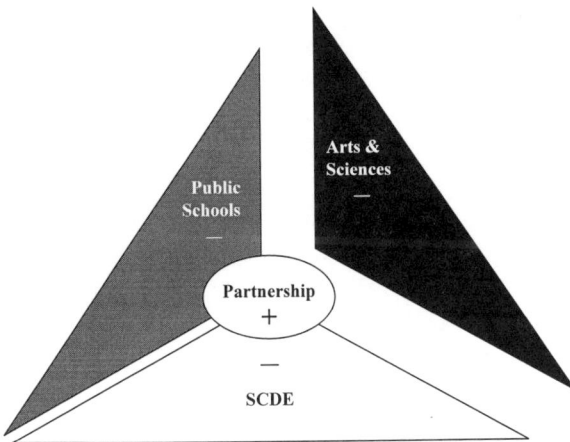

Figure A.4. The School-University Partnership (1980-1995)

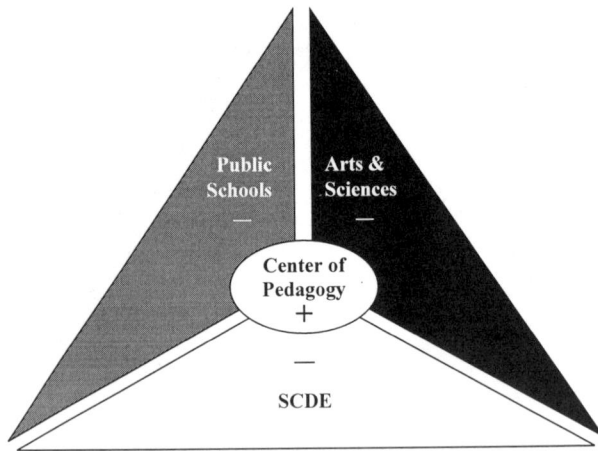

Figure A.5. The Center of Pedagogy (1995-)

sciences from the broader university. Such collaboration resulted in the creation of partner and professional development schools throughout the nation—places where pedagogical practice and theory could come together in a single location, resembling in some ways the earlier ties between theory and practice that existed in laboratory schools (see The Holmes Group, 1990; Osguthorpe et al., 1994).

Centers of Pedagogy

Although partner schools were essential to the educational renewal process, their establishment did little to involve arts and sciences faculty and foster campuswide commitment to teacher preparation. For this and other reasons, Goodlad (1994) began discussing the need to create "centers of pedagogy" that would include all three constituencies: a) teacher educators, b) public school educators, and c) arts and sciences faculty. Figure A.5 shows how such centers can be viewed as the organizational entities that attract the three disparate groups of educators together around the common purposes of improving teacher education and K-12 schooling. These centers, which are just beginning to emerge on campuses in the United States, are portrayed as having the potential to change the nature of the school-university partnerships in which they are established, the kind of potential that Goodlad was attempting to nurture when he held the initial seminar in 1992 and invited arts and sciences administrators to attend.

Examples of
Cross-Campus Collaboration

Science Education

The kind of collaboration that centers of pedagogy foster occurs in most school-university partnerships even before the centers themselves are established. As with most institutional change, organizational structures follow from new developments in organizational mission, goals, and functions. For example, years before the idea of a center of pedagogy was put forth, the Southern Maine Partnership initiated a project to improve K-12 science teaching by inviting professors of astronomy and physics to join with teacher educators and school faculty to redesign the entire science education experience (see Kimball, Swap, LaRosa, & Howick, 1995). Not only were campus courses affected by this broader sweep of collaborative effort, but field placement experiences were also changed so that campus teams with a variety of backgrounds supervised the students preparing to be teachers.

Art Education

When our university announced the construction of a new fine arts museum, the fine arts dean recognized the potential of the new museum to enhance the education of school children. To meet the needs of K-12 students, fine arts faculty collaborated with an interdisciplinary task force to design curriculum capable of making fine arts experiences meaningful to young students. The result was an integrated curriculum built around museum exhibits and experiences. Over 96,000 students and teachers visited one of the exhibits introduced and enhanced by these curriculum materials. Following their visit and study of the curriculum, many students returned to the museum and acted as guides for their parents and other family members.

Conclusion

The arts and sciences professors in the previous examples who joined with others to improve K-12 learning and teacher preparation programs were in a very real sense nurturing their disciplines, as well as their students and the pupils in the schools. Rank and tenure requirements at most institutions of higher education demand that faculty contribute to the research literature in their academic specialty. We believe that these same faculty should be committed as well to the ways in which their discipline is being taught to the young. Elementary and secondary school pupils who do not gain the deep interest in science or art that was experienced by many of the students who participated in the aforementioned initiatives will be much less likely to pursue these topics after they leave high school. And the less likely the young are to engage in serious study of a given discipline, the more vulnerable that discipline is to decline.

In his book *Scholarship Reconsidered*, Ernest Boyer (1990) calls for institutions of higher education to broaden their definition of scholarship to include the study of teaching. Centers of pedagogy provide a place for such study to occur. In these centers, arts and sciences professors, education faculty, and school educators can come together to improve K-12 learning, as well as the preparation of the next generation of public school teachers. Boyer focuses primarily on a scholarship of teaching aimed at instruction that welcomes the addition of K-12 teaching into his definition. With this addition, the other more traditional forms of scholarship will be nurtured simultaneously because students at all levels will develop greater interest in a field and have a stronger tendency to follow their interest until they have made their own contribution to the discipline.

We do not underestimate the challenge of effecting such changes in both higher education and public schooling. For collaborative ventures that involve arts and sciences faculty to endure, pedagogy will need to be valued more within the broader university—not only for how it can improve instructional quality on campus, but for how it can lead to a new generation of public school teachers who will be better prepared to serve the children and youth they will encounter in the K-12 classrooms of the future. Only with the greater commitment and direct involvement of arts and sciences faculties, such as those described in this chapter, will teacher education programs be able to achieve these goals.

The historical developments that have led to the creation of school-university partnerships, partner schools, and centers of pedagogy depict the continuing evolution of American education. Some might see these events as the results of nostalgic longings for an earlier era when teacher education was a less complex endeavor. But rather than returning to the past, these new institutional transformations are leading to educator preparation programs that not only bring more unity to theory and practice but create reflective educators in the process—educators who know their subject and how to teach it, but who also understand themselves and the contributions they are uniquely prepared to make in the classroom and beyond (see Bullough & Gitlin, 1995).

References

Barfuss, S. (1996). *Fieldnotes on a partner school: The effects of a cohort teacher education program on inclusion model of special education.* Provo, UT: BYU-Public School Partnership.

Beck, L. G., & Murphy, J. (1996). *The four imperatives of a successful school.* Thousand Oaks, CA: Corwin.

Beck, R. H. (1980). *Beyond pedagogy: A history of the University of Minnesota College of Education.* St. Paul: North Central.

Berry, D. L. (1985). *Mutuality: The visions of Martin Buber.* Albany: State University of New York Press.

Bly, R. (1996). *The sibling society.* New York: Vintage.

Bolman, L. G., & Deal, T. E. (1995). *Leading with soul: An uncommon journey of spirit.* San Francisco: Jossey-Bass.

Boyer, E. L. (1990). *Scholarship reconsidered: Priorities for the professoriate.* Princeton, NJ: Carnegie Foundation for the Advancement of Teaching.

Britsch, T. A. (1992, August). *Building upon strong foundations.* Addresses delivered at the 1992 annual university conference, Brigham Young University, Provo, UT.

Britsch, T. A. (1993, August). *Continuing toward excellence.* Addresses delivered at the 1993 annual university conference, Brigham Young University, Provo, UT.

Buber, M. (1950). *Paths in utopia.* New York: Macmillan.

Buckley, J. (1989, July 26). The hard lessons of school reform: The Rochester experiment. *U.S. News and World Report,* pp. 58-60.

Bullough, R. V., & Gitlin, A. D. (1995). *Becoming a student of teaching: Methodologies for exploring self and school context.* New York: Garland.

Carpenter, K. J. (1986). *The history of scurvy and vitamin C.* London: Cambridge University Press.

Clandinin, D. J., Davies, A., Hogan, P., & Kennard, B. (Eds.). (1993). *Learning to teach, teaching to learn: Stories of collaboration in teacher education.* New York: Teachers College Press.

Clark, D. (1996). *Schools as learning communities.* London: Cassell.

Clark, R. W. (1995). Evaluating partner schools. In R. T. Osguthorpe, R. C. Harris, M. F. Harris, & S. Black (Eds.), *Partner schools: Centers for educational renewal* (pp. 229-262). San Francisco: Jossey-Bass.

Clifford, J. C. & Guthrie, J. W. (1988). *Ed school: A brief for professional education.* Chicago: University of Chicago Press.

Clift, R. T., & Lou Veal, M. (1995). *Collaborative leadership and shared decision making: Teachers, principals, and university professors.* New York: Teachers College Press.

Cochran-Smith, M. (1993). *Inside-outside: Teacher research and knowledge.* New York: Teachers College Press.

Coles, R. (1993). *The call to service: A witness to idealism.* Boston: Houghton Mifflin.

Covey, S. R. (1989). *Seven habits of highly effective people: Powerful lessons in personal change.* New York: Fireside.

Covey, S. R. (1997). *Seven habits of highly effective families: Building a beautiful family culture in a turbulent world.* New York: Franklin Covey Golden.

DePree, M. (1989). *Leadership is an art.* New York: Dell.

DePree, M. (1992). *Leadership jazz: The art of conducting business through leadership, followership, teamwork, touch, voice.* New York: Dell.

Dewey, J. (1910). *The influence of Darwin on philosophy, and other essays in contemporary thought.* New York: Holt.

England, E. (1988). *The best of Lowell L. Bennion: Selected writings 1928-1988.* Salt Lake City: Deseret.

Fullan, M. (1993). *Change forces: Probing the depths of educational reform.* London: Falmer.

Fullan, M., & Hargreaves, A. (1996). *What's worth fighting for in your school.* New York: Teachers College Press.

Goldberg, D. (1991, May 19). Plains tour planned as modest monument to changing south. *Atlanta Constitution,* p. 4.

Goodlad, J. I. (1984). *A place called school: Prospectus for the future*. New York: McGraw-Hill.

Goodlad, J. I. (1990). *Teachers for our nation's schools*. San Francisco: Jossey-Bass.

Goodlad, J. I. (1994). *Educational renewal: Better teachers, better schools*. San Francisco: Jossey-Bass.

Goodlad, J. I. (1997). *In praise of education*. New York: Teachers College Press.

Greene, M. (1995). *Releasing the imagination: Essays on education, the arts, and social change*. San Francisco: Jossey-Bass.

Herrmann, B. A., Beaudin, L., Bird, B., Pierce, L., Draper, L., & DeWitt, P. (1996, April). *School-based collaborative inquiry: Creating communities of inquiring learners*. Paper presented at the annual meeting of the American Educational Research Association, New York.

The Holmes Group. (1990). *Tomorrow's schools*. East Lansing, MI: Author.

Hyde, L. (1983). *The gift: Imagination and the erotic life of property*. New York: Random House.

Illes, L. (1997). *Ecosystems and villages: Using transformational metaphors to build community in higher education institutions*. Provo, UT: Brigham Young University.

Kerr, D. H. (1997). Toward a democratic rhetoric of schooling. In J. I. Goodlad & T. J. McMannon (Eds.), *The public purpose of education and schooling* (pp. 73-96). San Francisco: Jossey-Bass.

Kimball, W. H., Swap, S. M., LaRosa, P. A., & Howick, T. S. (1995). Improving student learning. In R. T. Osguthorpe, R. C. Harris, M. F. Harris, & S. Brown (Eds.), *Partner schools: Centers for educational renewal*. San Francisco: Jossey-Bass.

Lopate, P. (1996). *The art of personal essay: An anthology from the classical era to the present*. New York: Anchor.

MacIver, R. M. (1924). *Community*. London: Macmillan.

Maizels, J. (1996). *Raw creation: Outsider art and beyond*. London: Phaidon.

Moyers, B. (1995). *The language of life: A festival of poets*. New York: Doubleday.

Myers, C. B., & Simpson, D. J. (1998). *Re-creating schools: Places where everyone learns and likes it*. Thousand Oaks, CA: Corwin.

Nathan, J. (1996). *Charter schools: Creating hope and opportunity for American education*. San Francisco: Jossey-Bass.

Nibley, H. (1989). *Approaching Zion*. Salt Lake City, UT: Deseret.

Noddings, N. (1992). *The challenge to care in schools: An alternative approach to education*. New York: Teachers College Press.

Noddings, N., & Shore, P. J. (1984). *Awakening the inner eye: Intuition in education.* New York: Teachers College Press.

Osguthorpe, R. T. (1996a, April). *Collaborative evaluation in school-university partnerships.* Paper presented at the annual meeting of the American Educational Research Association, New York. (ERIC Document Reproduction Service No. ED 398 223)

Osguthorpe, R. T. (1996b). *The education of the heart: Rediscovering the spiritual roots of learning.* American Fork, UT: Covenant Communications.

Osguthorpe, R. T. (1997). The power of the arts to edify. In D. R. Walling (Ed.), *Under construction: The role of the arts and humanities in postmodern schooling* (pp. 119-135). Bloomington, IN: Phi Delta Kappa Educational Foundation.

Osguthorpe, R. T., Harris, R. C., Harris, M. F., & Black, S. (1994). *Partner schools: Centers for educational renewal.* San Francisco: Jossey-Bass.

Osguthorpe, R. T., & Osguthorpe, R. D. (1996). Changer les pratiques éducatives par le partenariat: Une comparaison d'écoles partenaires en France et aux Etats-Unis. *Apprentissage et Socialisation, 50*(3), 61-74.

Palmer, P. J. (1993). Good talk about good teaching: Improving teaching through conversation and community. *Change, 25,* 8-13.

Paris, S. G., & Ayres, L. R. (1994). *Becoming reflective students and teachers: With portfolio and authentic assessment.* Washington, DC: American Psychological Association.

Patterson, R. S., & Osguthorpe, R. T. (1996, December). *Positive tensions: Keys to educational renewal in a school-university partnership.* Paper presented at the annual meeting of the International Council on Education for Teaching, Amman, Jordan.

Rennigner, K. A., Hidi, S., & Krapp, A. (1992). *The role of interest in learning and development.* Hillsdale, NJ: Lawrence Erlbaum.

Rogers, D. (1994). Conceptions of caring in a fourth-grade classroom. In A. R. Prillman, D. J. Eaker, & D. M. Kendrick (Eds.), *The tapestry of caring: Education as nurturance* (pp. 33-47). Norwood, NJ: Ablex.

Rowley, J. (1988). The teacher as leader and teacher educator. *Journal of Teacher Education, 39*(3), 13-16.

Sarason, S. B. (1982). *The culture of the school and the problem of change.* Boston: Allyn & Bacon.

Sarason, S. B. (1996). *Revisiting the culture of the school and the problem of change.* New York: Teachers College Press.

Schlichtemeier, K. (1996). *Creating school-university partnerships for educational renewal: A case study of the Brigham Young University-Public School Partnership.* Doctoral dissertation, University of California at Los Angeles.

Schrage, M. (1990). *Shared minds.* New York: Random House.

Sergiovanni, T. J. (1996). *Leadership for the schoolhouse.* San Francisco: Jossey-Bass.

Simpson, J. A., & Weinere, E. S. C. (1989). *The Oxford English dictionary* (2nd ed.). Oxford: Clarendon.

Sirotnik, K. A. (1994). Equal access to quality in public schooling: Issues in the assessment of equity and excellence. In J. I. Goodlad & P. Keating (Eds.), *Access to knowledge* (pp. 159-185). New York: College Entrance Board.

Stake, R. E. (1995). *The art of case study research.* London: Sage.

Stein, J., & Urdang, L. (1983). *The Random House dictionary of the English language.* New York: Random House.

Stewart, H. (1993). A search for identity: A retrospective view of the processes of formation of the Brock Faculty of Education Centre on Collaborative Research. In D. J. Clandinin (Ed.), *Searching for connections: Struggling for community* (pp. 14-21). Edmonton: University of Alberta, Among Teachers Community, Research for Teacher Education and Development.

Stewart, H. (1997). Metaphors of interrelatedness: Principles of collaboration. In H. Christiansen, L. Goulet, C. Krentz, & M. Maeers (Eds.), *Recreating relationships: Collaboration and educational reform* (pp. 27-57). Albany: State University of New York Press.

Strike, K. A. (1990). The legal and moral responsibility of teachers. In J. Goodlad, R. Soder, & K. Sirotnik (Eds.), *The moral dimensions of teaching* (pp. 188-223). San Francisco: Jossey-Bass.

Taba, H. (1955). *School culture: Studies of participation and leadership.* Washington, DC: American Council on Education.

Vajda, S. (1989). *Fibonacci & Lucas numbers, and the golden section: Theory and applications.* New York: John Wiley.

Van Galen, J. A. (1996). Caring in community: The limitations of compassion in facilitating diversity. In D. Eaker-Rich & J. A. Van Galen (Eds.), *Caring in an unjust world: Negotiating borders and barriers in schools.* Albany: State University of New York Press.

Young-Bruehl, E. (1996). *The anatomy of prejudices.* Cambridge, MA: Harvard University Press.

Index

CORWIN PRESS

The Corwin Press logo—a raven striding across an open book—represents the happy union of courage and learning. We are a professional-level publisher of books and journals for K–12 educators, and we are committed to creating and providing resources that embody these qualities. Corwin's motto is "Success for All Learners."